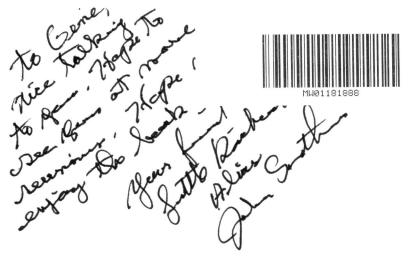

Scumbag Sewer Rats

Scumbag Sewer Rats

AN ARCHETYPAL UNDERSTANDING OF CRIMINALIZED DRUG ADDICTS

by

John E. Smethers, Ph.D.

Scumbag Sewer Rats: An Archetypal Understanding of Criminalized Drug Addicts
ISBN-10: 0-9551503-5-3
ISBN-13: 978-0-9551503-5-7
Published by CheckPoint Press, Ireland
"Books With Something To Say"

CHECKPOINT PRESS, DOOAGH, ACHILL ISLAND, CO. MAYO,
REPUBLIC OF IRELAND
TEL: 098 43779
EMAIL: EDITOR@CHECKPOINTPRESS.COM

WEBSITE: WWW.CHECKPOINTPRESS.COM

Cover design, book design and editing by CheckPoint Press

Registered with the US Library of Congress and the British Library

THIS BOOK IS DEDICATED TO MY DAUGHTER

LYNDA

FOREWORD

Most people separate alcoholism from drug addiction, workaholism, sex addiction, gambling, and overeating, etc. With that in mind, let's proceed with a short discussion on addictive behavior apart from the premise of this book. Does our parents' addictive behavior teach *us* addictive behavior? Is addictive behavior physiologically determined or genetic? Has society, through the media, contributed its share of the blame? Do our peers influence us? Is addictive behavior a result of coping mechanisms? Are we solely responsible for our own actions and behavior? Or, is it a combination of these—plus more. Most scholars in the field agree that it is a combination. Some researchers emphasize one over the others. It is my contention that there are *more* causes and dynamics going on than those discussed in this foreword.

Addictive behavior in parents often begets addictive behavior in their offspring. If a child grows up in a family in which one parent is an addict, the child is likely to develop an addiction. If both parents are addicts, the child's chances of addiction increases. Subsequently, the generational cycle of addiction continues. When adult children of addicts seek relationships, it is usually with people who are similar to them. This search doesn't usually happen on a conscious level. It is what Freud called 'repetition compulsion'.

It has been argued that the tendency toward addiction is biological, inherited genetically, or is a result of chemical imbalances. Cohen (1988) notes that "it is easy to postulate that the reinforcement centers in the ventral teg mentum, the locus ceruleus, the mediolateral frontal cortex, or the nucleus accumbens have an inborn deficiency of catecholamines or that the receptors are hyposensitive. Alternatively, perhaps the endogenous opioids are congenitally in short supply, or the delta opioid receptor is deficient in quantity or quality. Will diagnoses like 'hypoendorphism' or 'opioid receptor insufficiency' or 'hypodopaminosis' ever be made with reliability?" (p. 57). I wouldn't count on it.

Research reported by Kinney and Leaton (1995) suggests that heredity isn't as simple as was previously believed. At conception, we receive a unique set of genetic material—internal instructions that guide growth and development. These instructions set limits in the form of predispositions. The outcome will depend on unique life circumstances and the environment. Some people remain thin without effort and others put on weight easily (p. 80). This example of a genetic predisposition for weight-gain suggests that there is a genetic predisposition for addiction. How can we really know? The best that science can come up with is based on probability. Combined with life circumstances, addictive behavior is likely, which is giving credence to nature *and* nurture rather than nature *or* nurture. To complicate matters, the media among other causal factors, contributes its share of influence.

No one escapes the media's power to promote excess. Big business sell both gluttony and dieting, smoking, eroticism and an exaggerated need for the work ethic. Television commercials convey messages that encourage addictions in its audience. The commercial of a lady who puts her hand to her pain-wrinkled forehead and complains "Oh, this terrible headache," is generally seen in the next scene chipper and happy, thanking a miraculous wonder drug. Billboards with the Marlboro Man or Joe Camel have done their part in influencing us. Other influential media, directed at youth, is the glamorization of reckless lifestyles in movies. Kids grow up in a sea of advertising. Pre-adolescents see and hear beer and wine commercials exhorting them to drink before they are old enough. It can hardly be denied that the overall effect of advertisements is to glamorize whatever it is being sold, whether it is cigarettes, alcohol or over-the-counter medication, and to encourage the idea that what is being advertised will make them feel better or enhance their lives in some way.

It appears that life events may be mediating factors in the development of mental and emotional illnesses in general, and drug abuse in particular. What if dad's brother died? What if dad lost his job? What if dad had to serve a jail sentence? What if mom was an only child—not having the large-family experience, then grew up and had five children? What if she was a full-time housewife, belonged to the PTA, held a part-time job, and was expected to participate in civic activities? Could addictive behavior be a coping mechanism for life events such as dad's, and stress such as mom's? In Bratter and Forrest, Litz (1979) reported that within a group of alcoholics and nonalcoholics, the alcoholic group reported the impact of stress to a higher level than the nonalcoholic group (p. 77). These results can apply to pre alcoholic men and women also, creating a need to relieve stress. "It calms me down. It helps my nerves. It helps me unwind after a hard day." This explanation, says Kenny and Leaton (1995), can be viewed as the *anxiety thesis*. Partially a derivative of Freud's work, he stated that during times of anxiety and stress, people look to the past for things that worked for them. Theoretically, he proposed, the security of mom's breast as an infant can later influence the use of the mouth for eating, smoking and drinking disorders (p. 6).

During puberty and early adolescence there is a need for identity. Young people want to break from their parents. They fall into close associations with peers, and those peers have a profound influence. Peer pressure can also come from the workplace. Bratter and Forrest state that adolescent and occupational research both suggest that drinking is a learned behavior, and that it is learned from those who have the most social influence on the subject. To be included in certain subcultures, it is necessary to drink or use drugs (p. 14). Those who later develop drinking problems are likely to have started using alcohol at an earlier age than is typical for the general population. Also, the presence of a heavy-drinking partner has been found to increase both the amount and rate at which alcohol is consumed. Similar results in the number and rate of cigarettes smoked have been obtained from smokers exposed to a high-rate smoking friend as opposed to a low-rate smoking friend (p. 15).

Many members of 12-step programs claim that influences are only suggestive—it was *they* who made a voluntarily decision to drink or use drugs. Nobody twisted their arm and made them drink it. It is their contention that they alone are responsible for their actions. Suggested causes, to them, are excuses that gave them permission to drink or use drugs. In one of the stories in back of the *Big Book of Alcoholics Anonymous* (1991), a woman states, "the mental twists that led up to my drinking began many years before I ever took a drink, for I am one of those whose history proves conclusively that my drinking was a symptom of a deeper trouble." (p. 544).

These theories, et al, are what prevailing literature proposes as the causes and conditions of addiction. But I have come to believe that the term 'addiction' - especially in the early stages - is a misnomer when applied to all substance abusers. This is because most people who are thought of as addicts are not actually physically addicted, as the heroin *addict* is—most of them have what I have termed an *addictive mind-set and lifestyle*. What follows in Chapter One are depth psychological perspectives, and we'll explore more causal explanations for the *addictive mind-set and lifestyle* in Chapter Three.

Anyone who wants to know the human psyche will learn next to nothing from experimental psychology. He would be better advised to put away his scholar's gown, bid farewell to his study, and wander with human heart through the world. There, in the horrors of prisons, lunatic asylums and hospitals, in drab suburban pubs, in brothels and gambling-hells [sic], in the salons of the elegant, the Stock Exchanges, Socialist meetings, churches, revivalist gatherings and ecstatic sects, through love and hate, through the experience of passion in every form in his own body, he would reap richer stores of knowledge than text-books a foot thick could give him, and he will know how to doctor the sick with real knowledge of the human soul

C.G. Jung

CONTENTS

CHAPTER 1

ORIENTATION AND OVERVIEW

The orientation of this book is depth psychological. Depth psychology is a tradition initiated by Sigmund Freud, Carl Jung, and elaborated on by others, including James Hillman with his archetypal re-visioning of psychology, as well as the phenomenological schools of thought. The spirit of depth psychology is nourished by an understanding of and a participation with literature, mythology, spirituality and alchemy, as well as Eastern traditions and quantum physics.

Depth psychologist James Hillman is the founder of archetypal psychology, which is an understanding of human nature through the archetypes (*arche* means first, *typos* means mold or pattern)—or symbolic patterns. Depth psychology started with psychoanalysis. Under the rubric of depth psychology are psychodynamic psychology, analytical psychology, ego psychology, individual psychology, feminine psychology, *archetypal* psychology, transpersonal psychology, alchemical psychology, ecopsychology, terrapsychology, and liberation psychology, just to name a few. Jung's theory of the collective unconscious is an amalgamation of archetypes (that can be thought of as a gene pool of behavioral patterns in the psyche). Examples of archetypes include the martyr, the good mother or the bad father, the entrepreneur, and the criminal, to name a few. Before going into an *understanding of the lived experiences* of criminalized drug addicts through the archetypes, let's first briefly explore other depth psychological perspectives.

Woodman (1982) is convinced that the same problem is at the root of all addictions. The problem being different in each individual. The problem, whatever that may be, presents itself differently in different people (p. 9). Overeating, alcoholism, gambling, sex, drug addiction, etc., are all likely symptoms of an underlying cause. There are many causes, such as those discussed in the foreword—some proven and some theoretical, but others may never be known, and still more should be further investigated.

"Many of us, regardless of gender," says Woodman, "are addicted because we have been driven to specialization and perfection by our patriarchal culture. Obsession is at the root of perfection. An obsession is a persistent or recurrent idea, usually strongly tinged with emotion, and frequently involving an urge toward some kind of action, the whole mental situation being pathological" (p. 10). The roots of fear can also be pathological.

Without going into the many causes of fear, it must be considered a legitimate reason to lean on something for emotional support. If not properly bonded, for example, fear will most likely manifest in some way. This fear being unconscious, there is not a way to intervene. "The mother," says Woodman, "who is in this situation herself because of her own heritage, cannot give her baby the strong bonding to the earth that the mother grounded in her own instincts can" (p. 61). Fear is often anger in disguise, and anger often produces rebellious conduct.

Rebellion encompasses various types of behavior, which include criminality and addiction. Substance abusers are characteristically thought of as rebellious. What causes rebellion? A patriarchal society can cause rebellious behavior in women. Authority figures often create rebelliousness in both men and women. In contrast, recovery can be viewed as a form of rebellion against addiction. Therefore, rebellion does not have to be negative. Rebellion can result in healing. This form of rebellion is spiritual, and spirituality is an entity that needs to be developed. Addicts who personify the *puer aeternus* (eternal lad in Latin) and the trickster archetypes that we'll be elaborating on later, are typically rebellious individuals. Sometimes we can even rebel against ourselves.

Approximately a month before I was released from prison, I weighed more than I had in my entire life. Not knowing anything about fat, carbohydrates, or portion control, I started fast-walking around the prison yard *per diem*, every day. While I managed not to gain any more weight, I didn't lose any either. When I was released, I continued walking—usually ten miles a day. I didn't gain any more weight and I may have even lost a little. It was my *fantasy* to be slim and again have a size thirty waistline. My reason for wanting to lose weight was to improve my chances with women—a fantasy.

Most of us have mental arguments with ourselves when we're trying to make a decision. When my head suggested that I adopt a healthy lifestyle, I resisted because it would be too much work. I said to myself, "Self, I wouldn't have enough time; besides, exercising for health purposes would mean exercising and changing the way I eat permanently. All I want to do is lose some weight." My other self countered by saying "only thirty to forty-five minutes a day is all that is required." This dialogue in my head went back and forth until I finally lost the argument and continued doing what I was doing with minimal results.

It was much later that I came to realize that exercise and eating right is about physical expression, being healthy, feeling good, and longevity (imagination), and not about looking good (fantasy). How many exercise regimens fall by the wayside because the exerciser's motives was in the way because of a *fantasy*, rather than *imagination*?

Before becoming familiar with Imaginal Dialogues and Jung's concept of active imagination, I spent a lot of time talking to myself (out loud, I might add) when I was alone—usually at home or driving in my car. I still do this, but I have learned to apply this in a different way and benefit from it. These conversations are between me and someone else, usually someone I know. I am usually trying to convince someone, let's say my friend Jack, to accept my point of view about something; therefore, I have two people in my head in dialogue, and both of them have a point of view.

Previously, my description of this behavior was that I was just talking to myself. When this voice answered me, it was not my friend, the human Jack. It was my *image* of him. It was the Jack *in me* that answered. I then needed to place Jack in a didactic position, and allow him to argue his case. My friend Jack is very argumentative, so I had to really think in order to be able to replicate what he would say if he was really there. This process required nurturing, and I finally mastered it. Often I have to lose an argument to Jack to learn something. I don't always use Jack's image, sometimes it's Rich, and sometimes others. It depends on the issue. I also tried visualizing different images to represent Rich or Jack—rather than my visual image of them as people. Apparently, the "I" has very little control over the spontaneous thoughts and images that pop up. I am often able to accept Jack's and Rich's positions, or that of others, in order to come to the best conclusion. This is a form of active imagination called imaginal dialogues.

Prior to recovery, my *ex*ternal locus of control placed the blame for everything that happened to me—out there: she made me do it; if the cops would stop harassing me; if only, and I shoulda, woulda, coulda. In order to develop an *in*ternal locus of control, we all need to learn to ask ourselves what part we have played in it? whatever "it" is. Questioning our motives by using imaginal dialogues like I do with Jack and Rich, is a depth psychological practice that anyone can employ for any number of reasons.

Freud wrote of a similar method. He said that when he writes, he often used questions to challenge his own points. He answered the questions, then did it again, and again. By making sure there were not any other questions that could weaken his argument, the point he was making was strengthened and reinforced.

In Jungian psychology, active imagination is a way of assimilating unconscious material such as dreams and fantasies through various forms of self-expression. The object of active imagination is to give a unique voice to the personality's archetypal structures, such as the *puer* and trickster and especially the shadow, that are normally not heard, thereby establishing a line of communication between our conscious ego and the unconscious. Even when the end products, such as drawing, painting, writing, sculpture, dance, music, etc., are not interpreted (like dreams in Jungian psychology often are), something still happens between creator and his or her creation that contributes to a transformation of consciousness. Jung's contributions aren't given the attention that say, Freud's has, but I find them much more intriguing and useful than Freud's.

Part of a letter to Carl Jung published by the cofounder of Alcoholics Anonymous, Bill Wilson (1984), told Jung how the message reached Bill at the low point of his own alcoholism; the letter described his own spiritual awakening, the subsequent founding of A.A. and the spiritual experiences of its many thousands of members. As Bill put it: "This concept proved to be the foundation of such success as Alcoholics Anonymous has since achieved. This has made conversion experience . . . available on an almost wholesale basis." (p. 383).

Better known as the dark side of human nature, the shadow archetype is the primitive and usually unwelcome side of personality that derives from our animal forbears. Unconsciously we can sometimes project the shadow onto other people. Here is an example by Johnson (1991):

> A young Japanese girl in a small village became pregnant. The villagers pressed her to name the father. After many angry words, she finally confessed. "It's the priest," she said. The villagers confronted the priest. "Ah so," was all he said. For months the people were down on the priest. Then a young man who had been away returned and asked to marry the girl. He was

the father of the child. The girl accused the priest to protect him.
The villagers then apologized to the priest. "Ah so," he said (p.
38).

The girl projected her shadow onto the priest and the villagers. The
wise priest kept silent and the problem worked out well for everyone
concerned. This example demonstrates the shadow in an environmental
setting. Johnson also demonstrates this on a personal level using Marie
Antoinette:

> The bored queen decided she wanted to touch something of the
> earth and ordered milk cows so she could become a milkmaid.
> After the cows' arrival she found this distasteful and changed her
> mind. The Queen's original impulse was correct: she needed
> something to balance the formality of her court. If she would have
> continued as a milkmaid, the history of France might have been
> different. Instead she was beheaded (p. 54).

Marie tried to balance her highly refined life with some peasant
task, but she didn't see it through. If the shadow operates in the form of
the addictive cycle for years of one's life, then stops through the
recovery process, the constructive lifestyle afterwards can be a very
rewarding experience for the individual and the *Village*; therefore,
society and the addict can benefit from the shadow.

Spiritual experiences can be life changing and Jung's contribution
has since changed the lives of thousands of people. Oracular guidance
is also a spiritual experience. Oracular consciousness has to be
developed over time; therefore, if enough time isn't devoted in
developing it, what may be interpreted as oracular guidance may in
reality be some other unknown influence.

"Give me a sign, God!" How often have people, in one way or
another, sought guidance in this manner? A trigger for addictive
behavior can be pulled by stress or life events resulting in looking to the
divine for guidance. This trigger might also be pulled by seeking
oracular guidance. Skafte (1997) says, to receive an oracle is to receive
guidance, knowledge, or illumination from a mysterious source beyond
the personal self (p. 3). Skafte proposes that 'the shadow' may appear
in unexpected places when the oracle is sought (p. 136). Personality
traits and genetic idiosyncracies are omnipresent, as is the dark side of
our psyche. Relying too much on oracular guidance could lead to a road
that isn't conducive to spiritual needs. Something as unlikely as a bird
flying into a neighborhood tavern, could set into motion a possible

solution for a problem. Taking the bird's flight as an oracular signpost, a recovering addict might enter the tavern and find an old drinking buddy he hasn't seen in a long time. Thinking the oracle has again provided guidance, a relapse could follow. The justification for an addict to relapse is often irrational, and he certainly wouldn't admit that he followed a bird into a bar for a solution to a problem.

The personal unconscious, Jung (1959) describes as containing lost memories, painful ideas that are repressed (i.e. forgotten on purpose), subliminal perceptions, by which are meant sense-perceptions that were not strong enough to reach consciousness, and finally, contents that are not yet ripe for consciousness (p. 65). The collective unconscious may be thought of as an impersonal or transpersonal unconscious because, as Jung says, "it is detached from anything personal and is entirely universal, and because its contents can be found everywhere, which is naturally not the case with personal contents" (p. 65). A more simple definition of the collective unconscious, as previously mentioned, is thinking of it as a gene pool of behavioral patterns in the psyche; therefore, this theory is contradictory to John Locke's theory of *tabula rasa*—that of being brought into the world with a clean slate before it receives the impressions gained from experience. Said yet another way, Jungian psychology postulates an objective psyche, or collective unconscious, made up of forms, molds, and energies that serve as blueprints for common and universal human experiences. These are the archetypes.

Whether it is the more widely accepted stimuli discussed in the foreword, or the stimuli gleaned from depth psychology, or a combination of each, there are considerably more dynamics involved when it comes to addiction; therefore, depth psychological perspectives should be investigated more vigorously. A spiritual awakening like that of which Jung proposed to Bill Wilson, can lead to recovery, wiser choices, and a chance to become a more self-actualized human being.

As Hillman (1997) points out, the primary rhetoric of archetypal psychology is myth. This move toward mythical accounts as a psychological language locates psychology in the cultural imagination. Secondly, these myths are themselves metaphors, so that by relying on myths as its primary rhetoric, archetypal psychology grounds itself in a fantasy that cannot be taken historically, physically, literally (p. 28). Therefore, the archetypes cannot be proven anymore than dreams can. How can they, they're unconscious?

What follows is an exploration of two archetypes to understand the criminalized drug addict. These two patterns are the *puer aeternus*, and the trickster—a prominent figure in many world mythologies. This exploration argues that these archetypes are very familiar when we read about the flighty *puer* (pronounced poo-air) or the uninhibited trickster, we are bound to recognize behavioral patterns that remind us of people we know or are at least familiar with. Since these archetypes are primarily personified by males, we won't elaborate on the small percentage of women who fall into this category. The reasons will become evident.

The past offers a profound resource to prove that culture, as much as individuals, moves through predictable stages of development that mirror the course of natural evolution. Drug addiction and criminality also go through a developmental process. Though there isn't a specific, predictable evolution or developmental process for addiction that can be applied to all addicts, there is a prototype. Often addictive and criminal behavior evolve at the same time. Criminalized drug addicts for the most part, start evolving from habilitated pre-teens, to the stripling experimentation of adolescence, and on to the puerile behavior of adulthood, and finally into criminal activities, which is when they start personifying the trickster archetype. Indicating how an archetypal *understanding* of this evolution can illuminate the developmental history of drug use and criminal activity, is not to propose that socio or psychopathic criminal behavior is only in accord with the *puer* and trickster archetypes. We'll be exploring the world of the criminal mind in the following chapter.

However, *understanding the lived experiences* of criminalized drug addicts through the archetypes is the crux of this book. Don't we have a proclivity toward *understanding* when we root for the downtrodden, or for a likeable outlaw in a movie, such as *Harry Tracy—Desperado*, starring Bruce Dern (which is based on a true story, by the way). With the movie *Thunderbolt and Lightfoot* with Clint Eastwood and Jeff Bridges, the audience finds themselves wanting the robbers to get away with their crime. Of course, screenwriters and directors may tend to present some characters more sympathetically than others, but still it evokes *understanding* in the audience—we often identify with them. Jesse James was a folk hero, and so was the mythical Robin Hood. During the American Civil War, hero worship was bestowed on guerrilla fighters such as John Singleton Mosby, John Hunt Morgan, and Quantrill who were not only puerile and wily tricksters, but outright killers. More conducive to substance use is the sympathetic treatment of the high-flying *puerile* behavior of Peter Fonda and Dennis Hopper in *Easy Rider*. We in the audience are drawn to their foot-loose and free-wheeling lifestyle.

It is worth considering what can be learned about *criminalized* drug addicts that is different from the usual theoretical and statistical studies done on drug addicts in general, as discussed in the foreword to this book. Can a depth psychological perspective—specifically the archetypes in criminalized drug addicts, help us to better *understand their lived experiences*? Will this *understanding* of criminalized drug addicts help us to determine why they don't respond well to treatment, and why their recidivism rates are so high for prison and recovery? And what are the ramifications of criminalized drug addicts being viewed as, and viewing themselves as dirty, lying, cheating, scumbag sewer rats?

We will examine the lived experiences of drug addicts who have become criminalized, in varying degrees of misdemeanor and felony. As one who was once a criminalized drug and alcohol addict, I can attest that drug addicts believe that they are, and that they are viewed by others as dirty, rotten, lying, scumbag sewer rats, which suggests that a self-fulfilling prophecy could have causal implications.

To be sure, many criminalized drug addicts think of themselves within these cultural stereotypes. At a deeper level however, the lived experience of being a drug addict may be something quite different, and indeed, may vary from person to person. Certainly, many drug addicts seem to view themselves as victims; others may simply live in a minute-to-minute expediency as they search for their next bag; and some may even consider themselves to be misguided human beings who plan on quitting eventually.

It is common for adolescents or young men who think of themselves as hip, slick and cool, to start drinking and using drugs. Before they experiment with drugs, they usually don't have the motivation to indulge in criminal activity. Of course, poverty, bad parental role models, and a pressing need for cash can trigger criminal indulgence in anybody—criminal activity isn't restricted to only drug addicts. But most of these types of men will eventually succumb to drug use through association, if for no other reason that dealing drugs is good money. There are exceptions, but for the most part, it is a misconception (a myth) that drug dealers don't use their own products.

It is also difficult for many clean and sober addicts to change the con-artist ways they developed while they were using—conniving, lying, stealing, womanizing, and not being responsible or accountable for their actions. Just staying away from addictive substances isn't enough, so a majority of recovering drug addicts will repeat the same old behaviors and expect different results, which usually ends in relapse.

These individuals often start associating with their old buddies, hanging out in bars, and going to other hangouts. Many of them, such as speed and coke addicts, are accustomed to fast cash, fast women, and a fast lifestyle. It's very difficult for them to stay clean and sober. The same goes for the robbing and burglarizing night life of heroin addicts. These varied forms of criminal lifestyles are all they know. Drugs and alcohol offer a comfort zone they've been in, usually for the better part of their lives.

As one who spent many years with what I call an *addictive mind-set and lifestyle*, and associating with many criminalized drug addicts, I don't believe they are interested in causal explanations. They are too preoccupied with lying, cheating, and manipulating to satisfy the urgency of their next bag.

Generally speaking, drug addicts even lie when it would behoove them to tell the truth. For example, when a parole or probation officer asks them if they've been using drugs, most of them will instinctively lie even when telling the truth would be more likely to result in avoiding a violation of their parole or probation. Their lying will usually get them violated sooner than the dirty test.

Additionally, criminalized addicts often choose jail over treatment programs because the slammer is familiar; a place where they won't be expected to give up a lifestyle they've become accustomed to and comfortable with. Many addicts continue this compulsive behavior even though they suspect or even know that their reckless ways can lead to jails, institutions, and death.

If we consider the social problems that addicts cause, we cannot help but notice the financial and emotional grief that they inflict upon others. Not only do addicts cost taxpayers an astronomical amount of money, such as for medical care and for funding prisons, they also contribute considerably to the high morbidity and mortality in the culture due to viruses such as hepatitis B, C and HIV.

Many drug addicts hurt the ones they love the most, often by ripping off family members to buy drugs. How many families have learned the hard way that enabling addictive behavior by allowing an addicted family member to live with them most always ends with the stolen belongings of the family becoming profit for the fences (those who buy stolen property).

Burns (1999) integrates Jungian psychology and AA using

archetypal psychology in the treatment of alcoholism. He explains that merging archetypal psychology with twelve-step treatment has improved results at a lower cost. Burns explains that for us the principle door to the image is story. We use art, music, sports, and poetry, but the life story related in a gathering of people [such as meetings] with a similar experience provides the most economic access to the image. Sometimes we need to be reminded that the story is the fiction of the moment, the necessary illusion and *is* not the image, but *reveals* the image. Unfortunately the tendency is to interpret story, destroying both the story and the image. When a story session becomes boring that is generally what is happening (p. 19).

In Chapter Six, I include this often more-effective mode of elucidation; story—at least parts of my story, and some stories of others with the real-life component of dialogue between criminalized drug addicts. Personal experience through story is a valid research and reference tool. Qualitative researchers insist that qualitative methods are more appropriate than quantitative methods, allowing subjective knowledge. Knowledge gleaned from stories, whether fiction or otherwise, is a form of subjective knowledge. Academia is also recognizing that the personal experience of felons is proving to be a valuable teaching asset, thereby making it possible for this population to contribute to society rather than taking from it. However, there are those quantitative researchers who will forever discredit qualitative methods because of it's lack of scientific reliability and validity.

Quantum physicists however, have shown that accurate measurement can only be accomplished by including the effect an observer has on the object being measured. Said another way, we distort nature by excluding ourselves from the equation. Not including the effect our very presence has on nature is itself unscientific. It is a distortion of nature that produces a false representation of the real world.

In an article in the *New York Times*, Warren St. John (2003, August 9) discusses the role of ex-convict criminologist, professor Stephen C. Richards at Northern Kentucky University, saying that the time these professors spent as prison inmates adds special insight to their research and their teaching (A 13-15). My experience as an inmate in jails and prison, coupled with my background of addiction, adds a worthy component to the theoretical orientation of this book. However, my addictive mind-set and lifestyle and criminal background has been a disadvantage, rather than an advantage, in my repeated attempts to teach classes at colleges and universities.

We will never know how many addicts stopped their dope-fiend ways and lived out the rest of their lives as productive citizens— statistics are vague and negligible, as well as ever-changing. There are very few people whose lives have not been touched in some way by addicts, and the problems they cause to themselves are all too obvious.

Many people in middle-class and upper-class society visualize alcoholics as they are often depicted on popular media—derelicts stumbling down the street with brown paper bags in their hands. They often see drug addicts as thin, gaunt creeps with pale skin and scraggly hair, hanging out in alleys with tracks on their arms, lying around with dirty outfits (syringes) surrounding them. Within these stereotypes, addicts are thought of as degenerate, slothful, dishonest, hedonistic, and stupid *Scumbag Sewer Rats*.

Dishonest and hedonistic? Yes. Degenerate? Sometimes; but how can addicts be thought of as slothful when they will stop at nothing to get what they want—they are highly motivated when they want to be. And how can they be thought of as stupid and still have the creative intelligence that I will periodically discuss throughout this work?

The Alanon and Naranon programs are designed to help the families of addicts. According to the big book of Alcoholic's Anonymous (2001), the entire family is, to some extent, ill (p. 122). Family members will repeatedly give money to, lie for, and make excuses for their addicted relatives, mistakenly thinking that they're helping them. Regardless of the blinders that family members wear, most of them have a stereotypical image of drug addicts that certainly doesn't fit the image they have of their addicted kin. "Not my son!" Denial is obviously not restricted only to drug and alcohol addicts.

Recovery for extrinsic purposes, such as a nudge from the judge (12-step meetings or treatment), a spouse threatening to leave, or job security is rarely conducive to a lasting and productive recovery. Proclaiming themselves as hope-to-die dope fiends generally negates any and all attempts at intrinsic recovery. Most of these confirmed addicts are professionals at feigning recovery—even convincing themselves—for a while.

Why did they start using to begin with? The causes of drug addiction are uncertain, controversial, and many, as discussed earlier. Some scholars believe that addiction is a search for spiritual transformation. According to Corbett (1996), many symptoms such as addictions or sexual perversions, which were previously thought to be the result of intrapsychic conflict, and in theological literature thought to be "sinful," can now be seen to be attempts to counteract the sense of internal emptiness or chaos (p. 148).

William James (1958) refers to the consciousness produced by intoxicants and anaesthetics, especially by alcohol. He said the sway of alcohol over mankind is unquestionably due to its power to stimulate the mystical faculties of human nature (p. 324).

Weil (1972) states that the ubiquity of drug use is so striking that it must represent a basic human appetite. Weil also suggests that altering consciousness is innate. Perhaps the internal need to release inhibitions, be devious, act crazy, fight, gamble, chase women, lie, cheat and steal, is also an innate need to alter consciousness (p. 17). Maybe some people are destined to live by organizing principles that we are unaware of. There may be far more than we would like to admit that we simply don't know or *understand*. Perhaps many of our present theories are wrong.

During the course of this book, I will use my own developmental experience, first as a fledgling *puer* drinking on weekends and later experimenting with drugs, to becoming a criminalized drug addict. Often I will use mythology and examples from the lives of other criminalized drug addicts, and some experiences of famous people to illustrate that the addictive mind-set and lifestyle isn't limited to the lower socioeconomic classes. The archetypes do not discriminate and neither do drugs, alcohol, and criminality.

CHAPTER 2

THE FUN PHASE OF SUBSTANCE ABUSE AS *PUER AETERNUS*

Weekend warriors are known in the field of addictions as Periodics. They also refer to them as binge drinkers or users. Most people separate alcoholism from drug addiction. Although there are those who fully realize that alcohol *is* a drug, many of them nevertheless instinctively use the term 'alcoholic' when referring to alcohol *addicts*. Anyway, addicts such as myself commonly start as periodics, using only on the weekends because we were not allowed freedom on school nights. I went to a party when I was 12 years old and didn't get back until I was 45.

By the time I was 15, I had started climbing the lower rungs of the alcoholic ladder. During the summer of that year, I was jailed three times—none of which would have occurred if I had not been drinking. The first arrest was for curfew, the second for petty theft, and the third for driving under the influence of alcohol (DUI) on my Cushman Eagle motor scooter. As a result, my driver license was revoked before I got it. At that time, instruction permits were issued by the California Department of Motor Vehicles to those who were 15½ years old, providing they had successfully completed a driver training course. With an instruction permit, one could operate a motor scooter, or an automobile as long as he or she was accompanied by a licensed driver.

Thus was the beginning of more than 30 years as a practicing addict—first alcohol, then drug experimentation during the summer of my graduation from high school. Two years later I was arrested for my first drug charge—possession of narcotics, to wit—marijuana.

I started drinking not long after I entered junior high school, and it wasn't long before I was running with a pack of delinquent-prone kids. We drank for fun. Ending up hugging the toilet bowl the morning got after was the residual affects of the fun; therefore, not a deterrent. We got drunk before football games, school dances, and Friday nights at the movie theater. We seldom knew what the movie was about. Starting fights for no apparent reason was commonplace, and during those junior high days, we were even into malicious mischief such as breaking residential house windows and running; knocking on doors and running, and sometimes when the unsuspecting resident answered the door, we would plaster their screen door with a water balloon.

As I mentioned earlier, however, it wasn't until I was 15 that I finally landed in jail, but it was for curfew. I was drunk, and the officer could have booked me on a DUI charge on my scooter, but he didn't. The next morning I was released to my parents.

Two weeks later my friend Jimmy told his mom that he was spending the night at my house. I told my parents I was spending the night at his. Instead, we stayed out all night drinking Ripple wine on my motor scooter. About six o'clock in the morning when the Ripple stopped winking back at us, we started getting cotton-mouth. We then stole some milk off a porch, went to the high school and drank it, then busted the bottles on the steps of the main building. Minutes later we were taken to jail for petty theft—the woman in the house had seen us steal her milk, and reported us to the police. Again, the officer could have booked me on a DUI and for breaking those milk bottles, but he didn't. Again I was released to my parents.

Three months later they finally booked me on a DUI charge. "Damn those cops! The bastards were picking on me." And I really believed that. How many kids at that age have an internal locus of control? Very few. Most of us are going to point the finger outwards—blaming whoever or whatever is the most convenient.

I interviewed several drug addicts as a research method in an effort to *understand* how they viewed their addiction. Not using their real names, I will refer to them as Dasher, Dancer, Prancer, Comet, and Vixon.

These addicts discussed with me what it was like when they started using drugs and alcohol, and in a way they seemed to relive some of the pleasure of those times in their lives. All of them talked about how innocent their drug use was at first, saying that it was fun and exciting. This is the beginning *fun phase* of the developmental process.

Before we addicts built legacies of disgust, suspicion, mistrust, pity, and fear from society, we were just out to have a good time. A recurrent theme with the addicts I interviewed - which were all male - is that they initially responded by explaining what it was like when they started drinking or using.

They described their first years of *using* as fun. They elaborated on this extensively before they began talking about their descent into the netherworld of addiction. Most of them began by talking about their early experiences. There was one exception—Dasher, but he still kept within the *fun* theme.

Dasher commented, "Well, it's been my experience that addicts have a tendency to elaborate extensively on the good times, and not so much on the bad times."

Dancer said: "I'd describe it as starting out as a lot of fun. It started out as a big party, and I started out right away getting high every day, every chance I got, and that was when I was about 13 years old."

Prancer followed: "Well, my addiction started off real innocent, just smoking pot, stealing beers from dad out of his refrigerator and that was, like, in junior high and it wasn't really a problem. It was just, you know, it was fun."

The same goes for Vixen: "Well, they were good experiences. I mean, when I first started off using, you know, it was not a big deal. I mean, we're partying, we're drinking, we're using, we're whatever. Early on it was exciting."

Comet said: "I loved my addiction. I loved the use of drugs. It started off as very pleasant. I enjoyed it." These guys talked about those initial years of experimentation as though they thought at the time that they could go on like that for the rest of their lives, and they probably did think that. I know I did.

Normal human development allows for the sewing of wild oats. So by the time one enters their twenties, maturation usually starts taking place, and one starts developing a sense of responsibility and account-ability. We're supposed to pursue education, career, and/or get married and start a family. Or, many of us stay trapped in an adolescent stage. Teenagers usually live in the now. Practicing addicts also live in the now. Emotionally, addicts behave like teenagers and are often described as adolescent in behavior and attitude. After all, many of the issues that they grapple with are the same as with teenagers. The difference is that addicts stay trapped in an adolescent stage for as long as they live with the addictive mind-set and attitude. This describes the addict, but it also describes the *puer aeternus*.

Archetypally, this syndrome is referred to by von Franz (2000) as *The Problem of the Puer Aeternus*. In her book, she says that "the man identified with the archetype of the *puer aeternus* remains too long in adolescent psychology; that is, all those characteristics that are normal in a youth of seventeen or eighteen are continued into later life" (p. 7).

The *puer* (the female counterpart is *puella*) archetype has been around *ab ovo* and will live on *ad infinitum*, as with all archetypes. This one has a dual nature, however. The dual archetype of the *puer aeternus* is in *conuinctio* (conjunction) with the *senex* (old man in Latin) and has a bipolar *complicatio*—positive and negative *puer* and positive and negative *senex*. The negative sides can be thought of as the dark or shadow side of our personality.

As with all archetypes, their interpretations often change. Therefore, von Franz gave her interpretation of the *puer* when she wrote it. For example, in the original lectures later to be turned into the book cited above, she stated, "the strange thing is that it is mainly the *pueri aeterni* who are the torturers and establish tyrannical and murderous police systems. So the *puer* and the police-state have a secret connection with each other; the one constellates the other" (p. 164). von Franz doesn't mention the *senex*. James Hillman's interpretation however, does. I will address Hillman's dual-archetype interpretation later, which does coincide with von Franz' statement about the police state.

Drug abuse and addiction came of age in the 1960s. As with many other social phenomenon, the *puer* has come of age concomitantly. What I mean is, I am interpreting contemporary *puer* phenomenon as coinciding with the emergence of the drug culture of the early '60s. It should be noted of course, that *puer* psychology can also be present unattached to addictive processes, and addiction can occur without the personification of the *puer* archetype. Generally speaking however, the two, since the 60s, are inextricably linked.

Currently, drug and alcohol experimentation occurs simultaneously, rather than sequentially—as it was with me back in the fifties. The pre or early teen years being the focal point of demarcation, lasting from two to ten years; I have come to label this period as the *fun phase* of substance abuse.

This beginning fun phase is usually a result of some type of peer influence. Leroy Street, a heroin addict at 15 years old, also attributes peer influence to initial drug use. Street, back in 1953, said what is still true today: "I never knew anyone who became an addict all by himself. Behind every new 'dope fiend' is an older one who for one reason or another brings the neophyte into a group for what might be called established addicts" (p. 6). Sure, it is unlikely that a youngster in early adolescence is going to score from someone established in the drug environment without first being introduced. Many addicts and dealers won't have anything to do with young teens—their lack of experience makes them untrustworthy and loose-mouthed. They have a strong tendency to brag.

Kiley (1983), author of *The Peter Pan Syndrome* says, "they desperately need friends. Many of them turn to drug abuse, sexual promiscuity, and other vices in a fruitless search for rescue" (p. 83). Peer importance is paramount in adolescent psychology. Parents lose priority and peers become their crutch, their mainstay, their ever-present source of *adolescent self-actualization*.

According to Frankel (1998), "the yearnings of the adolescent substance abuser evoke the image of the *puer*. Substance use produces a state of mind that frees one from responsibility. Getting high offers *experiential transcendence* [italics mine]—the high flying puer, soaring through the spirit world" (p. 210).

The negative pole of the *puer* is characterized by a poor adjustment to daily demands, a failure to set realistic goals and to make lasting achievements in accord with these goals, and a habit of intense and short-term relationships with women. The positive pole of the *puer* is characterized by noble idealism, creative imagination, spiritual sensitivity, and often by extraordinary talent. Ironically, sometimes these positive and negative attributes emerge simultaneously.

Puer figures are found in mythology. Narcissus, for example, was a handsome youth who fell in love with his own reflection in a stream of water and then stayed there, pining away until he died. He was the object of the passions of many girls and nymphs but he was indifferent to them all. The nymph Echo fell in love with him but she could get no more from him than the others. When the rejected girls asked the heavens for vengeance, Nemesis heard them and lured Narcissus to the stream where he met his just due.

Dionysus, noted for being the god of the vine and of wine (and why not other chemical substances?) and of mystical ecstasy, was transformed by Zeus into a child to keep his wife, Hera, from recognizing him. Later, as a *puerile* man, he introduced his revels in which the whole populace, especially the women, were seized with mystical ecstasy.

Whereas I will elaborate more on Lenny Bruce in the next chapter, his *puer* disposition cannot be ignored. For example, according to Goldman (1974);

> "Lenny and a couple of friends were hanging out one day and he grabs his friends' arms and drags them across the street. There, in front of a huge pinball arcade was a big battered sign that read *Hubert's Museum and Flea Circus*. Excitedly, Lenny says, 'Look, man, isn't this fantastic!' Before them is the

> world's largest collection of old war-surplus fun machines;
> bell-flash pinball, ramp-thump skeeball, see-saw rocking
> pony, racing car windshield look out. Also, there's a Gypsy
> fortune teller, blue-flash-green-curtain foto [sic] booth,
> western badman, creaky-dopey candy crane, submarine
> torpedo kill-the-Japs, knuckle-white grip tester, and an old-
> fashioned shooting gallery, crammed with all those corny
> ducks and profile tanks and twerpy soldiers" (p.27).

Lenny's callow excitement is reminiscent of the typical salad days of innocence, and his excitement is genuine; however, also genuine is his inclination for the sick and deranged. Goldman continues, denoting the outlandish proclivities of Lenny's early career:

> After allowing his friends one good look at this fun jungle with
> its spider monkey, Lenny hauls them through the uproar to the
> back of the arcade. In a little booth, filling it like a coil of
> sausages in a box, sits an enormous woman selling tickets off
> a roll. Lenny buys three, hula-hulas through a turnstile and
> descends headlong down a very steep flight of stairs. It's like
> tumbling down a coal chute into another world. The whole
> Alice-in-Wonderland thing turned sordid and sick. A Platonic
> underworld of freakiness. Standing around this large subterra-
> nean chamber, elevated like statues on their tiny spotlit
> stages, are all your archetypal freaks. Sealo, the Seal Boy.
> Andy Potato Chips, the Midget. Estelline, the Sword
> Swallower. Congo, the Jungle Creep. Princess Wago and her
> Pet Pythons. Presto, the Magician. John Hailey, the Strong
> Man. Jean Carol, the Tattooed Lady (p. 27).

Lenny's excitement is innocent enough, but his ecstatic fascination with the freaks is another thing. His comic ingenuity and wit were phenomenal in the world of show business, but the subject matter from which he chose to deliver it was twisted for the times.

More consistent with the positive *puer* is the mythological Peter Pan who makes no bones about not wanting to grow up. But more realistic examples are the noble idealism of student rebellions; the pranks and antics of practical jokers and cartoonists; the extraordinary talent of race-car drivers, magicians, and sports figures; and the creative imagination of fairy tale authors such as James M. Barrie and Lewis Carroll. And we can't leave out Hollywood's most representative *puer*, Robin Williams.

Being an archetypal configuration of its own, the *puer* is paired with the *senex*. *Puer aeternus* (eternal boy) and *senex* (old man) is the configuration of the dual *puer/senex* archetype. The *senex* archetype originates in the Greek god Saturn-Kronos, (Kronos is the Greek word for time). Hillman (1970) explains that "Saturn presides over honest speech—and deceit; over secrets, silence—and loquacious slander; over loyalty, friendship—and selfishness, cruelty, cunning, thievery and murder" (pp. 154, 155). Old man *senex*, however, is usually constellated after the *puer* has run its course. When *puerile* men who recover from their addictions finally start growing up, they then start personifying the *senex*. We lose some of our flighty *puer* ways and start getting down to business - for the most part that is - for the *puer* never really goes away.

Cited earlier, von Franz stated that the strange thing is that it is mainly the *pueri aeterni* who are the torturers and establish tyrannical and murderous police systems. So, when Hillman says, "the *puer* and the police-state have a secret connection with each other; the one constellates the other," they are basically saying the same thing. von Franz just doesn't include the *senex* pole of the dual archetype.

Hillman continues: "He is the just executioner and the criminal executed; *the prisoner and the prison* [emphasis mine]. He makes both honest reckoning and fraud" (pp. 154, 155)." Again Hillman's correlation to von Franz is obvious. *Senex* duality presents moral values inextricably meshed with shadow; good and bad become hard to distinguish.

I have known people in 12-step programs who have become members of the American judicial system—usually as probation officers rather than police officers. Many recovering addicts *would* become police officers if their police records didn't prevent them. On the other hand, alcoholism and drug addiction is common in most police departments.

"Because of the inherent antitheses," says Hillman, "a morality based on senex consciousness will always be dubious. No matter what strict code of ethical purity it asserts, there will be a balancing loathsome horror not far away, sometimes quite close—in the execution of its lofty principles. Torture and persecution are done in the best of circles for the best of reasons: this is the negative *senex*" (pp. 154, 155).

It is not uncommon knowledge that there is a fine line between the character of criminals and the character of law enforcement officers. They are alike in many ways. The same can be said of parole and probation officers and prison guards. Hillman and von Franz has also articulated this observation, but Hillman further developed *puer* theory to include the *senex*—a well thought out re-interpretation, but I will use the words of a retired police officer to further demonstrate the correlation these authors were making between the archetypal and the police state.

I attended a forum where panelists were giving talks about prison, each coming from their personal or professional perspectives. The panelist we're concerned with here, was a former Los Angeles police officer—rampart division. Gil's *mea culpa* promulgated a *modus operandi* that generally does not get talked about—especially in public and on videotape. As a law enforcement officer, his credentials are impressive, which includes being a qualified gang expert and narcotics expert. My intention is to demonstrate a parallel between cops* and criminals, sometimes using parts of Hillman's previous quote concerning Saturn to help elucidate *puer et senex*.

Gil Contreras (2000) said that "there is a universal *cop culture*." He said that during his reign as a police officer, they functioned very much as hunters. For example, they would act like victims to get criminals to commit a crime against them, then other officers would jump out of the bushes, beat them up, arrest them and take them to jail—*lupus est homo homini*—man is wolf to man. "Saturn presides over honest speech—and deceit," said Hillman. Police officers, deceitful as they often are, also perform honorable service, for "he makes both honest reckoning *and* fraud."

Gil stated that they actually didn't mind shooting people at all. "Saturn is the just executioner and the criminal executed," said Hillman. We know that the life of a cop often ends in a paroxysm of violence. We also know that gang life on the streets often ends in violent death. The violence of each group (and the similarity of their thinking) is congruent with their respective codes of ethics, *silent leges inter arma*—the laws are silent amid arms. Cicero once said that when one's life is threatened by violent plots and the laws have been reduced to silence, one has the right of self-defense in any way possible.

Cops make their jobs personal, devoting their lives to it; therefore, the shady side of their jobs they view as exculpatory—they do it with impunity. Gil said that cops act very much like gangs: each have uniforms, each have their own codes they talk in, each have belief systems about right and wrong—both being very rigid, each tends to be

---

* Around 1700, perhaps borrowed from Dutch, cop became a slang word meaning 'to get ahold of, catch, capture.' This word is unusual because slang words usually either die or become respectable-it is still a slang word. *Copper* is one who cops or catches criminals. Ironically, drug addicts have adopted this word for *'copping'* drugs.

uneducated—most street cops are high school graduates or GEDs, each are closed societies—viewing people that are not a part of it as outsiders. Outsiders, stated Gil, don't need to know that we're out there hunting criminals. Most outsiders are not aware of the Augean* stables of many police departments.

The scandalous behavior of one of Gil's partners was that of arbitrarily starting fights for various reasons, one of those reasons being to see what his partner would do. In other words, to see if they could trust Gil not to report his partner's violence to their superiors. Gil said that during his law enforcement years, he knew that the things he was doing were wrong but he felt inviolable. However, we have to ask ourselves, how much good did he do over the years that he spent as a police officer? "Senex duality presents moral values inextricably meshed with shadow; good and bad become hard to distinguish. Because of the inherent antitheses, a morality based on *senex*-consciousness will always be dubious," says Hillman. "No matter what strict code of ethical purity it asserts, there will be a balancing loathsome horror not far away, sometimes quite close—in the execution of its lofty principles" (pp. 154, 155). Gang bangers have the reputation for being bad, but human nature tells us that there is inherent good in all people; therefore, we have the same dichotomy as we do with police officers.

"When debriefing," Gil said, "we often drank alcohol until five o'clock in the morning." Police officers have a high rate of alcoholism *and* drug addiction. Since cops are usually hired right out of the community, finding prospective police officers that have not experimented with drugs and alcohol is difficult, so hiring them is often an imbroglio. Drugs and alcohol are part of cop culture; drugs and alcohol are a part of gang culture; and drugs and alcohol are a large part of the criminal element in general.

Police officers also have a high suicide rate. "His eyes droop with depression, apathetic to all events," says Hillman, "and they stare inconsolably open, the super-ego eye of God taking account of everything" (pp. 154, 155). Unfortunately, teenage depression and subsequent suicide are one of the highest causes of death among that age group.

The same can be said about correctional officers. Reutter (2007) explains that "investigations, arrests, suspensions and firings of numerous Pennsylvania jail employees prove a claim that is often made

---

* Augeas, the mythical king of Elis, kept great stables that held 3,000 oxen and had not been cleaned for thirty years—until Hercules was assigned the job. Hercules accomplished this task by causing two rivers to run through the stables.

by prisoner advocates: Prisoners are no different than most people except they've been caught while others, who may be just as guilty of criminal acts, haven't. Put more succinctly, there is a thin line between the keepers and the kept" (p. 6).

Like the kept, the keepers are consistently in trouble. As Clarke (2007) points out, "the number of New Jersey state prison system employees terminated for disciplinary reasons rose from 33 in 2005 to 69 in 2006. 52 of the 2006 firings are final; 17 are on appeal. The reasons for the firings range from beating prisoners without provocation and allowing prisoners to attack other prisoners to smuggling drugs and cell phones in to prisoners. Guards also mishandled weapons, both on and off duty. One discharged a shotgun in the armory while another drove drunk with a firearm on his lap. A third, who was off duty at a bar, decided to spray a fly with Mace, making a bar patron ill" (p. 26). The 33 firings in 2005 and the 69 in 2006 were just the ones who got caught. It staggers the imagination to come up with an accurate figure of how much abuse is really going on.

A historically demonstrable personification of the *per/senex* archetype can also be found in the old West, which shows how the archetypes are recognizable at any point in history. Often we read about outlaws turning into sheriffs or marshals. Wyatt Earp comes to mind. According to the Time/Life series of *The Gunfighters* (1976), Wyatt and a friend had been charged with stealing horses; they were indicted by a grand jury, but Wyatt fled before the case came to trial. Then Wyatt started personifying the *senex* when he worked as a policeman in Wichita, Kansas, and later as marshal in the Tombstone Territory of Arizona (p. 16). Cops make their jobs personal, devoting their lives to it; therefore, the shady side of their jobs they view as exculpatory—they do it with impunity, and it doesn't matter whether it's in contemporary society or back in the 1800s when Wyatt Earp was slinging his gun and getting drunk in the saloons with the drunks and whores.

So, we find that the fun phase coincides with the *puer*, and the *puer* isn't necessarily restricted to those potential addicts often characterized by a low socio-economic background. The *puer* is also alive and well among the rich and famous. By the time he made *Less Than Zero* in 1987, Robert Downey Jr. had developed a serious drug problem. He reportedly began using drugs when he was eight years old, when his father, among others, introduced him to marijuana. He completed a drug-rehabilitation program in 1987 but continued to struggle with his addictions. By the time the 27-year-old Downey had come to be seen as one of the most gifted actors of his generation, he had also earned a reputation as a troubled and controversial figure in Hollywood.

Satinvoer (1980) points out that the *puer* strikes others as being narcissistic. The *puer's* introversion is engaged in a ceaseless effort to maintain the experience of the childhood 'self', and they will choose external circumstances—drugs, brief affairs, intense physical or mental activities—that enhance this experience. They will appear inordinately sensitive, and are liable to radical and sudden shifts in self-esteem (p. 75).

In reference to the *puer*, Kiley (1983) describes the victim of *The Peter Pan Syndrome* as;

> ...usually associated with drug abuse. Despite his pursuit of perfection, he is plagued with a nagging sense of worthlessness. This stimulates the need for relief. Since so many of his friends are engaged in drug abuse, it is easy for the victim to capitalize on the expanded consciousness that is typically associated with drug use. Excessive consumption of beer and marijuana becomes a regular habit. In more severe cases, cocaine becomes the one-way ticket to inviolate feelings of perfection (p. 127).

The rampant use of methamphetamine in recent years also holds sway over a deranged form of perfectionism.

Despite his tenuous legal situation, Downey managed to complete a number of films during the late 1990s. His probation was revoked in December of 97; however, after he was found to have used drugs again, Judge Mira sentenced him to six months in jail. Downey served 113 days of that sentence, during which he was allowed to leave several times to complete work on his film projects. Hmmm, I wonder what's going on with that? Looks to me like preferential treatment because of his Hollywood status.

Anyway, what a lucky break—back to Neverland where he has an endless round of adventure and freedom. While in many ways a land of light and liberation, Neverland is not without an admixture of evil, violence and cruelty. However, on Peter Pan's island (or Hollywood), "evil actions that an ethical ego must surely abhor, such as Hook's massacre of the Indians, the deaths of the pirate crew, and the attempted death-by-drowning of Tiger Lily, rarely evoke sorrow, remorse or suffering" (Yeoman, p. 108). Neverland and Hollywood, like the world of the fairy tale, is amoral, a timeless realm of an unending cyclical process in which there appears to be little consciousness of pain or progress.

Downey is a classic example of those who have remained trapped in *puer* psychology long after their adolescence was over. I was personifying the *puer* archetype until I was 45 years old, and this is not unusual. Many *puerile* men die in old age without ever achieving emotional maturity.

There are more archetypes working in many of my examples, but the one personified the most when criminalization becomes manifest in drug addicts, is the trickster. This mythological figure encompasses many different social positions, is utilized by different societies to inculcate various types of behavior, and may have manifold modes of appearance even within one culture. And the same goes for the *puer*. However, the rest of this book will focus more on the trickster, but the *puer* will always be there helping, goading, and influencing the trickster (and vice versa) when the need arises for a little *puerile* inspiration and some lofty ideals.

CHAPTER 3

WHEN THE FUN IS OVER
AND PSYCHOPATHY

The shift from the beginning fun phase, characterized by the addictive mind-set and lifestyle, to addiction, varies between individuals. And remember, we're still not talking about a physiological addiction. For the most part, it's psychological addiction. The average progression from early adolescence takes much longer because they usually have to live within the constraints of parental guidance, school, and all the responsibilities commensurate with that age group. Transition time is much shorter for adults because they're not as acquiescent to wives, employers, or the judicial system as they were to their parents. Keep in mind that this shift doesn't happen the same with everyone—circumstances can cause youngsters to accelerate their involvement with drugs and alcohol, and the road to addiction for adults can take a longer route. My progression was a typically slow one.

When I was 18, I was sentenced to 60 days in the San Bernardino county jail (Glen Helen Rehabilitation Center) for possession of alcohol by a minor and having an open container in a vehicle—30 days on each charge. Shortly after my release, one of my friends asked how I liked it. He was just kidding, but I will never forget his reaction when I smiled and said, "I liked it."

Compared to what I was expecting, I *did* like it. Two of my friends came into the same institution with me a couple weeks later. One of them was even assigned to the dorm I was in, and we also worked on the kitchen crew together. The other was in another dorm with only the day room between us, and at that time we were allowed to visit each other's dorms during day-room hours. We met new drug connections, played practical jokes on each other, and spent our off time talking about all the things we were going to do and how high we were going to get when we got out. I remember correlating my experience to being in a summer boy's camp. Glen Helen later gained the sobriquet, Camp Snoopy.

From that time forward, doing time was not much of a threat to me. In fact, I returned to Camp Snoopy four more times and eventually state prison. Over the years, 40 arrests landed me in local jails or in the county jail awaiting bail. Criminal charges ranged anywhere from curfew to armed robbery—most of which however, were substance-related charges. The ones that weren't listed as such, were linked to drugs or alcohol in one way or another.

The addicts I interviewed told me that between fun and addiction is when they started getting into trouble. They would pick up a DUI or a possession charge, or they would get suspended from school or fired from a job. Each made a statement concurring that none of these problems deterred them from continuing their drug use. My contention was—going to jail periodically was the dues I had to pay in order to sustain my quotidian need for drugs and alcohol.

During this shift, we still have fun, but it starts being compromised with problems. For example, when I was 20 years old, I got my second DUI. I managed to beat it in a jury trial, but I wasn't so lucky with the five succeeding DUIs that I incurred over the next 20 years.

Comet confessed that they asked him to leave the armed forces because of his addiction: "I was let out early because of my drinking and using." Prancer said: "I got fired from that job and then I said, fuck it, getting high is going to be my new job."

I can't remember all the jobs I was fired from or from which I quit. I was once fired for drinking on the job, and I was fired from another one because I was caught sleeping off a hangover. Sometimes these things start happening at a young age, especially those of us who started when we were 11 or 12 years old. For example, Prancer explained: "Before I got to the ninth grade, I got kicked out of school three times from three different schools and then they ran out of schools to send me to."

Of course bars are where we tricksters are usually 86'd from. Take Lenny Bruce for example, he was banned from Las Vegas clubs and eventually banned from night clubs nationwide. In his early career, Goldman (1974) tells us about the time:

> Lenny was in a Los Angeles nightclub called the Blue Angel. While doing his *schtick*, Lenny took a cigarette out of his pocket and started tapping other pockets looking for a light. "Excuse me, sir, would you be good enough to let me have your cigarette?" The spotlight fell on the giant black basketball player Wilt Chamberlain sitting at a ringside table. Standing, he reached up easily to Lenny's level on stage. Lenny lit his cigarette. He stared at Chamberlain's cigarette and examined the end of it closely. In an astonished tone, he confided to the audience: "*He nigger-lipped it!*" The audience was struck dumb, and there was an interminable silence. Suddenly, Wilt Chamberlain doubled over with laughter, slapping his big bony hand against his thigh. Sammy Davis Jr. then threw his head back and screamed with laughter (p. 47).

Was Lenny personifying the *puer* or the trickster? I'd say he was being more *puerile* than tricky this time, but the following con was before he made it as a stand-up comic, and definitely places him squarely in the trickster's court:

> Lenny put an ad in the *Los Angeles Times*: "Lenny, The Gardener, will clean, mow and edge your lawn for $6." At that time the standard price for the same job was $15, so, naturally, he had every moocher in the city calling the number in the ad. He'd take the first call and go roaring out to the address. Arriving rather breathlessly at the front door, he'd say, "Look, my truck just broke down. Do you have any equipment?" Then he'd take the equipment out and spread it all over the yard, maybe turn up a couple of spades of dirt. Then he'd say, "Look, I've got to go down to the store. I haven't eaten all day. Could you pay me now, and then I'll come back and finish?" When the people came across with the six bucks, Lenny, The Gardener, would split. According to Lenny, "I could do ten of those a day." (pp. 150, 151)

Perhaps this shift from fun to addiction is partly determined by the physiology of pleasure and pain. Pleasurable sensations diminish as they are repeated. The second piece of coconut-cream pie never tastes as good as the first one, and if you keep eating more it can become downright nauseating. On the other hand, pain and suffering become more and more exquisite with repetition—the more pain the more pain. The poet Keats said it this way: pleasure is oft a visitant, but pain clings cruelly to us. This becomes noticeable when considering the chaotic life of Lenny Bruce.

In my early twenties, I embarked on a career that involved unethical sales practices in service stations. My compeers and I sold tires by pinning (poking holes) and honking (cutting) the tires of travelers who came in for gas. We also sold shock absorbers, fan clutches, and fuel pumps by squirting oil on them and telling customers they were leaking. This confidence game rendered the *puerile* tricksters performing it 50 per cent of the profit; the other half going to the station owner.

Having been a lube bay bandit for several years, I don't believe I would have been characterized as criminally insane or a psychopath. I had needs, legitimate and illegitimate, and my determination to sustain my addiction prompted me to personify the trickster archetype which gave me the means in which to support those needs. Having run the gamut of drug abuse during my life, my story of *physical* addiction is unique in that I wasn't addicted to street drugs. I was a pharmaceutical addict for several years without having physicians writing prescriptions for me. *I was writing them myself.* Having been a lube bay bandit for well over ten years, and writing and running 'scrips for about ten years—not to mention my string of arrests, I'm sure there were those who suspected that I was bordering on criminality to the point of insanity; therefore, at this point, I'm going to expound on psychopathy and it's relationship to criminalized drug addicts.

PSYCHOPATHY

As we have seen, often the distinctions are minimal or nonexistent between *puer* psychology and the emergence of the trickster, because the fun-loving *puer* can himself be a little tricky. However, once addiction sets in, compounded with periodic trips to jail, negative trickster psychology starts to manifest. Archetypal personification in accord with developmental phases of addiction and criminalization aren't always in unison. There are hard-core, criminal addicts out there that have long passed being merely *puer* and/or trickster, and have evolved into antisocial personality disorder (also known as psychopathy)—which is the DSM's description of what used to be referred to as the criminally insane.

The difference between a psychopath and a sociopath is indistinct. The DSM-IV places both together under antisocial personality, because of their similarities. There are psychologists, however, that insist that there is a difference other than the similarities. I'll be using the terms psychopathy and psychopath rather than antisocial personality and sociopath.

Psychopathy consists of a group of character traits and behaviors, which includes irresponsibility, impulsiveness, hedonism, greed, egocentricity, and a pronounced lack of guilt, remorse or shame. Psychopaths are selfish, callous, and will habitually exploit others. They often become involved in socially unnatural behaviors. These behaviors appear in psychopaths without the signs of psychosis, neurosis, or other types of mental deficit found in other mental disorders. Psychopaths make up approximately 15 to 20 percent of the criminal population.

In comparison, addicts are also irresponsible, impulsive, hedonistic, greedy, and egocentric. Unlike psychopaths, however, they're not without guilt, remorse or shame, which is the major difference between the two. Depending on many variables, there are *puerile* and trickster behavior in psychopaths, and vice versa. Addicts are also selfish, sometimes callous, and often exploitative in their use of others, and depending on their drug of choice, will participate in socially deviant behaviors. Addicts make up approximately 70 percent of criminal populations and are responsible for as much if not more crimes and violent acts than even psychopaths.

The personality structure and life history of the psychopathic are quite different from those whose psychopathy is related to an emotional disturbance, and from those of a person whose psychopathic behavior results from living in a criminal subculture or in an environment in which such behavior is expected or rewarded, such as the criminal behavior resulting from addiction. Unlike the psychopath, these individuals are capable of forming strong affectionate relationships and of experiencing concern and guilt over their conduct.

The unadulterated criminal [psychopath] approaches the world with a sense of ownership, says Samenow (1989), as though people and objects are mere pawns on his personal chessboard. He aims to control other people just to enhance his own sense of power. Human relationships are avenues through which he pursues conquests and triumphs. The criminal expects others to do whatever he wants without hesitation. He delights in arguing for the sake of arguing. He is intent on winning what he regards as a battle, no matter how trivial the issue. This type of individual is a master at ferreting out weaknesses in others and ruthlessly capitalizing on them. When people oppose him, he can be merciless. Nearly everything he does, he does to feel powerful (pp. 14, 15).

The 'criminal' cited in the previous paragraph can be either psychopathic, or a criminalized, (usually male), drug addict. Obviously, there's not a fine line that designates which behaviors are relegated to psychopathy, and which behaviors are relegated to addiction. There's overlap, and much of it depends on the individual. There are addicts who have elements of psychopathy, and of course there are a great many psychopaths who are chemically dependent. One way to test it, I suppose, would be to observe an addict after he got clean and sober, and then observe whether or not he continues his criminal obsession. Perhaps then we could eliminate addictive substances as being causal.

Psychopaths are usually loners. Although they associate with people they *call* friends, it's not possible to really know them. They are pathological liars. Even the lies that are seemingly senseless make sense when one understands their motives. When they believe they are getting over on someone, they feel that they have the edge. Every time they get away with something, it excites them. These attributes aren't as fixed in addicts as they are in psychopaths. So much depends on the duration of addiction, drug of choice, and personal history, not to mention socioeconomic and cultural backgrounds, and of course which archetypes are dominant. The shadow archetype is often present in criminalized drug addicts, but the *puer* and trickster is prevalent. In psychopaths, the shadow is always prevalent.

Psychopaths take but rarely give without an ulterior motive. These people don't know what trust, love, or loyalty is. If they can gain something for themselves, they will indiscriminately betray their best friends. These people are so focused on pursuing their immediate objectives that they don't care a whit about what others think, nor do they consider their feelings. Invariably, they hurt those who care about them most. In one way or another, the psychopaths' mothers, fathers, brothers, sisters, spouses, and children all become his victims with no feeling of remorse—none.

A majority of the chemically dependent who display some of the above characteristics, if they do target their families, will usually have remorse. This remorse usually ends up on a fourth step if they ever make into the recovery process.

Herrnstein and Wilson (1985) emphasize that to a criminal [psychopath], life consists of a series of essentially unrelated events in which he seeks immediate gain and a buildup. He plots and connives, but rarely plans. With a winning personality, the criminal gains the trust and confidence of others and then preys upon them. Even the most cold-blooded criminal regards himself as a decent person. A man who had killed two police officers commented with complete sincerity that just because he murdered a couple of people, he was not a bad person

(p. 218, 219).

The DSM flatly states that the diagnosis of antisocial personality disorder (psychopathy) must not be applied to anyone under the age of eighteen; furthermore, the DSM will only categorize an adult over 18 as an antisocial personality. Instead, the term "conduct disorder" applies to children. It takes time for personalities to gel, and it is important not to mislabel a juvenile in a manner that might be harmful. The DSM doesn't state anything about age concerning substance-related disorders. Nowadays children are drinking and using drugs younger and younger, and it is not uncommon for parents to turn their kids on to both alcohol and/or drugs. There are pros and cons concerning psychiatric labels, but their use often conceals far more than they reveal and are open to misinterpretation. However, what is important is how a child is functioning—how he or she behaves and perceives themselves and the world.

As often happens with many personality disorders, say Carson and Butcher (1992), the causal factors in antisocial personality are still not fully understood. The perspective is complicated by the fact that the causal factors involved appear to differ from case to case, also from one socioeconomic level to another. Contemporary research in this area has variously stressed the causal roles of constitutional deficiencies, the early learning of antisocial behavior as a coping style, and the influence of particular family and community patterns (pp. 286-289).

We've established that causal factors in substance-related disorders are not fully understood, and the reasons are consistent with those in the preceding paragraph. Also, the problem with chemical dependency is further complicated by so many conflicting theories such as the nature/nurture controversy. However, let's compare some of the more accepted causative phenomenon of psychopathy to those of addicts.

BIOLOGICAL FACTORS

Because a psychopath's impulsiveness, acting out, and intolerance of discipline tends to appear early in life, several investigators have focused on the role of biological factors as causative agents. Research evidence indicates that a primary reaction tendency typically found in psychopaths is a deficient emotional arousal; this condition presumably renders them less prone to fear and anxiety in stressful situations and less prone to normal conscience development and socialization.

Behaviors that lead to the taking of drugs are gradually strengthened through operant and classical conditioning processes and by biochemical changes in the brain. What do we do when we do something we like? We do it again! We like the way drugs make us feel, so we do it again.

STIMULATION SEEKING

In a study of psychopaths, it was reported that they operate at low levels of arousal and are deficient in autonomic variability. These character- istics suggest a 'relative immunity' to stimulation, which would likely prompt them to seek stimulation and thrills as ends-in-themselves.

There are those who contend that altering consciousness is innate. Chemical substances certainly alter consciousness. However, like I stated earlier, perhaps the internal need to release inhibitions, be devious, act crazy, fight, gamble, chase women, lie, cheat, and steal is also an innate need to alter consciousness. Endorphins, a biological substance produced by the brain, also alters consciousness, hence the runners high.

GENETIC INFLUENCE

This sociobiological theory assumes a genetic influence or predispo- sition for particular behaviors. The validity of this view is not conclusive; however, I suppose it could provide some interesting leads for positivistic researchers to follow in further studies. Perhaps the most popular generalization about the development of psychopathy is the assumption of some form of early disturbance in family relationships.

The nature side of the nature/nurture controversy contends that alcoholism is genetic. Whereas I don't support that theory, it's more likely that a predisposition to addiction is more probable than a addictive predisposition to a specific substance such as alcohol. Therefore, the controversial gene is more likely to manifest in any number of addictive behaviors, such as drug or sex addiction, overeating, gambling, shopping, etc.

PARENTAL REJECTION, INCONSISTENCY, AND CHILDHOOD

Two types of parental behavior foster psychopathy. In the first, parents are cold and distant toward a child and do not allow a warm or close relationship to develop. A child who imitates this parental model will become cold and distant in later relationships. The second type involves inconsistency, in which parents are capricious in supplying affection, rewards, and punishments. Usually they are inconsistent in their own role enactments as well, so that a child lacks stable models to imitate and fails to develop a clear-cut sense of self-identity. When parents are both arbitrary and inconsistent in punishing a child, avoiding punishment becomes more important than receiving rewards. Instead of learning to see behavior in terms or right and wrong, the child learns how to avoid blame and punishment by lying or other manipulative means.

If parental rejection and inconsistency is so prevalent with psychopaths, then how could it not be so with the chemically dependent, at least to some degree? Perhaps the severity of this neglect is a determining factor. Let's survey what other researchers have to say in this area.

"Conventional wisdom," McGuire (1993) reminds us, "claims that if a youngster has serious problems, the parents must be the source. This point of view was prevalent for decades. Some children at a preschool age have characteristics that predict later crime" (p.12). Preschool aged children also have characteristics that predict addiction, but they aren't as easy to separate because those same characteristics also predict crime and other types of aberrant behavior. It's also assumed that if a child is raised by alcoholic or drug-addicted parents, then those parents are the source of their youngster's problems with addictive substances later in life. If the parents are not substance abusers, and the youngster turns to drugs and/or alcohol later in life, then the source for that dependency, and the characteristics that predict it, aren't as easy to identify.

As Samenow (1989) points out;

> The daily experiences of millions of parents, as well as a body of psychological research, suggest that the child is not a passive receptacle. Rather than haplessly being shaped by his surroundings, he himself shapes the behavior of others too. Two researchers in the field of child development have pointed out that any credible model of child development must consider the child as an active agent in social transactions. Any parent of more than one child knows that children differ in temperament from birth. One infant may be fussy, irritable, and restless; another may be docile and content. Isn't it natural for a parent to respond differently to a cranky, colicky baby than to a cooing, passive one? Whereas most parents *try* to raise their children with love and to provide them equally with opportunities, they invariably treat each differently. It could not be otherwise for, from birth, children have different temperaments, personalities, and needs (p. 29, 30).

Wilson (1992) talks about conventional wisdom when he stated;

We thought we knew all the answers: Children are wholly the products of their parents. We now know that the child brings a great deal to the parent-child relationship. Many aspects of personality have genetic origins, and some infants experience insults and traumas—ranging from lead poisoning to brain injuries—that makes rearing them a challenge to even the most competent parents. Two children in the same family often turn out differently. This casts great doubt on the notion that the shared environment of the children is the principle— or even an important factor in their development (p. A 40).

A form of infantile trauma that isn't discussed much in the literature is birth trauma. For example, when I was born, the attending physician used forceps to pull me out of the womb. Upon entering the world, my mother and I were both dead for over a minute—at least our hearts had stopped beating for that long. The team managed to resuscitate us. I was left with part of my head crushed in from the use of forceps. Could the trauma I experienced at birth have predisposed me to addiction later in life? According to psychiatrist Stanislav Grof (2000), yes:

The amount of emotional and physical stress involved in childbirth clearly surpasses that of any postnatal trauma in infancy and childhood, with the possible exception of extreme forms of physical abuse. Various forms of experiential psychotherapy have amassed convincing evidence that biological birth is the most profound trauma of our life and an event of paramount psychospiritual importance. It is recorded in our memory in minuscule details down to the cellular level and it has profound effect on our psychological development (p. 31).

If one were a fly on the wall in the office of a psychologist, one would hear juvenile offenders blame their parents, and parents blame themselves for their youngsters' misconduct. As many of these boys and girls realize just how vulnerable their parents are to feelings of guilt, they will level increasingly serious accusations against them. And so mothers and fathers who already doubt themselves as parents become even more guilt-ridden, depressed, and often angry with each other.

Take early school experiences. Poor performance in school is one of the strongest correlates of misconduct; however, what explains school performance? One possibility is that teachers label some children as troublemakers and slow learners and treat them in ways that becomes a self-fulfilling prophecy because they internalize what they're being told.

Another is children with low IQs who find school work boring and frustrating and turn to physical activity, such as acting out in the classroom. This also applies to those with considerably high IQs.

SOCIOCULTURAL FACTORS

Psychopathy is thought to be more common in lower socioeconomic groups. Although constitutional and family factors have been emphasized, it appears that social conditions such as those found in our urban ghettos also produce their share of psychopaths.

This is also consistent in drug and alcohol studies over the years, but there are considerably more addicts—especially alcoholics, in the higher socioeconomic groups—at least more so than with psychopaths. Considering everything just discussed about psychopathy, addiction, causes and conditions, is it any wonder that both groups find themselves locked up in penal institutions. Focusing now on addiction, consider Robert Downey Jr's battles with the law:

Downey's drug problems continued to plague him, and his legal troubles were just beginning. In June 1996, he was stopped for speeding, and policemen discovered crack cocaine and heroin in his car, along with an unloaded firearm. He was arrested again a month later when he was found passed out in a house in Malibu, California, just several blocks from his own residence; and again just three days after the second arrest, when he walked out of a drug treatment center where he had been ordered to stay. In November of '96, Superior Court Judge Lawrence Mira sentenced Downey to three years probation and fined him $250 after the actor pleaded no contest to drug and weapon possession.

In November of 2000 Downey was again arrested, this time in a Palm Springs hotel room, and charged with felony drug possession after police allegedly found cocaine, Valium, and methamphetamine in his room. Downey's trial, originally set for late January, was delayed for several months while his lawyers negotiated with prosecutors. In March 2001, the two sides failed to reach a plea bargain, and the case was set for a preliminary hearing at the end of April.

On 24 April, Downey was arrested for allegedly being under the influence of an undisclosed "stimulant". Officials later confined him to six months in rehab for violating his probation. Downey was reportedly fired from his job on *Ally McBeal* on 25 April, as producers decided to wrap production on the final episodes of the season without the actor. Downey's lawyers reached an agreement with prosecutors that required Downey to plead no contest to cocaine-related charges. He was sentenced to three years probation; the ruling allowed him to continue live-in drug treatment instead of returning to prison (biography.com).

I have elaborated so extensively on Downey's problems with the criminal justice system because it is so typical of how criminalized drug addicts spend a large portion of their lives. I went through that ongoing battle with the system for more than 30 years. Between July 1960 and January 1991, when I was released from parole, there was scarcely a time when I wasn't on probation or parole, doing time, community service, paying fines, pending court, or on the lam. I've been arrested more than 40 times for various misdemeanor and felony offenses—very few of which were unrelated in some way to my drinking and drug use.

As Hillman (1979) points out, the wounded leg or foot calls for a crutch. We need someone to lean on, special inclines, footstools, wheels. Winged and frail as the *puer* figure may be, he still can dominate through the power of his neediness (p. 104). Yes, we are usually unable to stop using on our own—we need help. We also need friends to lean on. It's ironic that such needy people are so independent—the *puer* and the trickster are often a paradox.

Downey's drug involvement has placed him in jail, but most of us today wouldn't label him as a psychopathic criminal. The same with Lenny Bruce. The criminal justice system, the shadow, the *puer,* and the trickster are bedfellows, and often the institutions where the *puer* and trickster are confined serves as a breeding ground for more sophisticated crime. It's doubtful that Downey suffered the negative influence of the criminal minds that he was incarcerated with—his financial income as a popular Hollywood actor kept him from entering the world of burglary, robbery, and other hustles. At least, he isn't known to have been arrested for such crimes. I believe it would also be safe to say that he personifies the *puer* more so than the trickster.

I don't mean to single Robert Downey Jr. out, for the *puer* addict is common in the entertainment industry, especially with musicians. Hank Williams, Elvis Presley, Janis Joplin, Jimmy Hendrix, and Jim Morrison (to list them all would take another book) never grew up and all died as a result of their addictions. These, and all the other entertainers that personify the *puer* archetype usually don't need to personify the trickster. Their professions provide enough funding for their addictions. They can *play* music or *play* parts in movies, they're professional lives are infolded into *puer* structure. Some entertainers don't personify the duel *puer et senex* archetype in sequence (old man *senex* is usually constellated after the *puer* has run its course). Comedy teams such as Laurel and Hardy offer a good example. Stan Laurel was the serious, practical *senex* off-screen, and the funny and zany *puer* on-screen.

Of course, when the *pueri* use their proclivities for criminal activity to support their chemical indulgences, the inevitable brushes with the law will land them not only in jail until they can post bail, but also serving time in county jails and state and federal prisons where they will be educated by the more experienced inmates—the felonious tricksters.

CHAPTER 4

FROM THE PARTY TO THE PRISON

T he years prior to the 1960s had a different type of criminalized drug addict, but their population was minimal compared to today. The population I am referring to are those drug (alcohol is also a drug) addicts before, especially during, and after the bootlegging years of prohibition:

Walker (1999) tells us a trickster tale about a unique saloon called the Dugout.

> It was located in a cellar between Red Mountain and Johannesburg astride the county line. Half of the saloon was in San Bernardino County and half in Kern County. Whenever the owner received a tip that a raid was coming from one county, he would move the liquor stock across the room into the other county. This worked real well until someone got their wires crossed and both counties raided simultaneously (p. 19).

This is a good example of what Hyde (1998) reports when he wrote that a trickster often gets snared in his own devices (p. 19). Walker tells another trickster story that took place in the Muroc area around Lancaster:

> A typical Muroc *still* was like the one near the Rich section-house. The road ran up toward the cattle pen where the cows stayed for the night. A prohi [called revenuers elsewhere] coming up the road at night would just see a dead-end road at the cattle pens. In the daytime, the wife, Mrs. Norma Rich, "a cowgirl by nature," took the cows out grazing, covering the

moonshiner's night truck tracks. Husband Max Rich kept guard on the little hill with a ladder up to a platform in a joshua tree. From there he could see for miles (p. 112).

Keeping on the lighter side for now, consider the following trickster story from Hyde about coyote:

> There is a great deal of folklore about coyotes in the American West. One story has it that in the old days sheep farmers tried to get rid of wolves and coyotes by putting out animal carcasses laced with strychnine. The wolves, they say, were killed in great numbers, but the coyotes wised up and avoided these traps. Another story has it that when trappers set metal leg traps they will catch muskrat and mink and fox and skunk, but coyote only rarely. Coyotes develop their own relationship to the trap; as one naturalist has written, "it is difficult to escape the conclusion that coyotes . . . have a sense of humor. How else to explain, for instance, the well-known propensity of experienced coyotes to dig up traps, turn them over, and urinate or defecate on them? (pp. 20, 21)

Coyote is a recognized trickster, especially in native American mythology. The above antics of coyote can be compared to the antics at the end of the following story told to me by my friend Comet when I interviewed him. Comet said,

"Psycho and I were going down main street. In those days I kept a 44 magnum under the seat of my truck. While sitting at a red light, Psycho saw some guys he had a beef with, and he reached under the seat and grabbed the gun. Before I had a chance to say anything, Psycho started shooting at them."

"Knowing Psycho, that doesn't surprise me a bit," I said.

"Yeah, we know how he got the name Psycho, huh? Anyway, I said 'now you've done it you fucking moron, the cops are right on our ass!' So the chase was on. After a reckless chase through a residential neighborhood, the cops finally got us cornered."

"The gig was up, huh?" I asked with a laugh.

"Yeah, but that's not all, John. Fortunately, the truck wasn't registered in my name. I hadn't changed over the title and registration yet. So I threw open the door, and there the police were with guns drawn." As I was getting out of the truck, the gear shift slipped into reverse, and because the idle was set so high, the truck took off backwards and hit the police car. Apparently, the squad car was in neutral instead of park, so the open doors on the police car knocked the cops down. That's when I took off running. As soon as I was out of their sight, I slid underneath a parked car, instead of having them chase me. Fortunately, it worked."

"Once the cops got their shit together, they took off running in the direction I had gone. Can you believe it, man? I swear, in the dark those cops didn't even see me—they ran right past the car I was layin under. I could see them running down the street from under the car. I also saw them split up, probably hoping to catch both of us. I stayed under the car for awhile in a panic, and after awhile I realized that I needed to find a rest room—fast."

"Why couldn't you just piss under the car?"

"No, John, I had to take a shit."

"Oh."

"Anyway, I rolled out from under the car and started to run in the opposite direction of the cops, but then I stopped next to the squad car—the door on the driver's side was still open. Then I saw the proverbial lightbulb above my head."

"What do you mean?"

"Well. I went up to the open door, dropped my pants, and dropped a load right on the driver's seat of the police car?"

We both laughed, then I said, "you gotta be bullshittin me."

"I swear to God, Bro, but check this out. Before I left, I rolled down the windows and closed the door of their car, so the smell wouldn't be so strong and they wouldn't see it. I was so proud of myself that I couldn't resist hanging around to watch what would happen. There just so happened to be a big tree nearby, so I climbed way up there and watched."

"Damn, you were askin to get busted."

"I know, but I couldn't resist. Anyway, when they came back, they had Psycho in handcuffs and they put him in the other police car that arrived on the scene. After the cops chatted for a while, one of them opened the door and got in. He reached out to close the door, but changed his mind and reached under his seat to see what he had sat on. Oh man, you shoulda heard him, John. He yelled: "GOD DAMN! SON OF A BITCH!""

We laughed again and I said, "I can't believe it. I'd give anything to see that."

"Hey, it was great! That cop jumped out of the car acting like he didn't know what to do with his hands and still cussing a blue streak. He was beside himself, Bro. I have never seen anyone in that much of a rage. How I kept from laughing out loud while I was up there in that tree, I don't know."

"I don't either," I said still laughing.

"John, we're not the only ones who thought it was funny." His fellow officers started rolling in laughter when they figured out what all the commotion was about. Watching their fellow pig clean off his hand and not knowing what to do with all that shit in the police car, they started cracking jokes like: 'Hey Mark, don't you carry toilet paper with you?' As the officer in the other squad car was pulling away, he stuck his head out of the window and said, 'Hey Mark, you wanna use some of my wife's perfume?' Then another officer said, 'Hey Mark, you better catch that scumbag or it'll be you that's arrested for defacing government property.'"

I laughed again and said, "And you were up in that tree watching the whole thing."

Considering this scatological story, I suppose Scumbag Sewer Rat was an appropriate handle for Comet in those days. However, compared to the stories told by many, we find a plural sensitivity inherent in the lives of most criminalized addicts (Jointsters, as I will refer to them periodically from now on). Many of these stories, in or out of prison, are funny. Others are pitiful, some abhorrent, and some can stir a range of emotions.

When I was 43 years old I was sentenced to the California Department of Corrections because of a probation violation that I received on a drug-sale case. Little had changed since the 1960s—with me and my blasé attitude about doing time, with my friends, or with the people I was incarcerated with at Camp Snoopy back then. The progression of my addiction was well advanced by this time.

I discussed the differences in the population of criminalized addicts prior to and after the 1960s. There is also a marked difference between prison populations prior to and after the '60s. The '60s is when the convict became the inmate.

The convict, the psychopath, and the gangster stereotypes are not mutually exclusive. Their acerbic personalities are often described as hardened, violent, racist, devoid of compassion, destructive, untrustworthy, and more. Is it any wonder that so many people in our society want to keep them locked up for their turpitude?

In the 1950s Humphrey Bogart and Fredric March played escaped convicts in a thriller entitled *The Desperate Hours* where they held a terrified family hostage. More recently Robert DiNero has portrayed similar figures in films such as *Goodfellas, True Confessions*, and *Cape Fear*. Whereas their roles are fictional, there are those in real life who are found on the front pages of daily newspapers, in magazines, biographies, case studies, newscasts, and documentaries about serial killers, pedophiles, rapists, cannibals, sadists, and many other people who have committed atrocities. These people have always and will continue to be housed in prisons—as it should be.

Thomas Gaddis (1955) provides an excellent example. He was the author of a book entitled *Birdman of Alcatraz* about Robert Stroud, which is what inspired the 1962 movie of the same name. The Hollywood portrayal made him look like an American folk hero with his scientific discoveries in medicine and his compassion for birds, but in reality he was quite different from the movie portrayal.

Jolene Babyak (1994) paints a more accurate picture of him:

> On November 1, 1911, Stroud struck Henry in the back with a knife. As Henry ran, Stroud got off a few more thrusts. A physician reported that Henry received seven stab wounds in his back, shoulder, upper arm and buttocks, one of which penetrated the pleural cavity. Stroud later admitted that 'he had intended to kill Henry and regretted being unsuccessful.' It was Bird Man's intention to kill two other prisoners too. Stroud was also a homosexual who proudly called himself a pederast, a man who prefers sex with boys (p. 62).

The MMPI confirmed a previous diagnosis of a "profoundly and significantly disturbed personality, a 'psychopathic deviate' who was impulsive and paranoid—the perfect profile of a sociopath" (p. 252).

Gilligan (1996) quotes Dennis X who intended to "gouge out his eyes, cut off his ears, cut out his tongue, cut off his penis and testicles, and then stuff all these up his anus" (p. 80). He was unable to complete that project only because the knife broke. Following the murder, "Dennis X experienced no feelings of guilt or remorse" (p. 80). This is the description of the psychopath described in the previous chapter.

The violence described above is what Fromm (1973) considers malignant aggression: "Cruelty and destructiveness, is specific to the human species and virtually absent in most mammals; it is not phylogenetically programmed and not biologically adaptive; it has no purpose, and its satisfaction is lustful" (p. 25).

The 1960s era is symbolic of the ending of the convict, but there are many who have failed to recognize this. The 1960s is when the convict started transforming into the inmate. Ironically, it was around this time that the term *inmate* was supplanted with *convict*. This period of transformation was earmarked by the proliferation of people being incarcerated—directly or indirectly—from charges resulting from the widespread use of, and addiction to chemical substances: *malesuada fames*—hunger that urges people to crime. The convicts prior to the '60s were incarcerated for the most part, for criminal activity without the impetus of chemical dependency. Since the 1960s however, prisons house mostly inmates who are there—directly or indirectly—from substance abuse and addiction.

The recidivism rate is high; the typical inmate will be back in the joint on a violation or with a new beef sometimes within months, and then the revolving door process continues. A buddy I grew up with began his addiction to heroin when he was about 22 years old. Before this, Jack had served several county jail sentences that were alcohol related. One of those sentences was in Camp Snoopy with me when I was there the first time. Because of armed robberies, burglaries, petty and grand thefts, under the influence charges, and other drug-related offenses, he has spent approximately 25 years in prison. Currently he's serving life without parole, thrice. He got the 3rd strike three times— that's 25-to-life three times. Prior to that sentence, not once did he ever take the first step toward recovery.

Consciously, most of us think we do not want to get caught, but unconsciously our behavior is saying, "Catch me, so I can go back home where I will be taken care of and provided for." How is a person made to prepare for a law-abiding life on the outside? In no way really. By taking away responsibility by being placed in the prison system, the inmate becomes less responsible. His self-reliance is atrophied. There is no understanding and no rehabilitation. Here is a conversation I had with one of my bunkies when I was at the Chino Guiding Center (now called Reception): "What are you going to do when you get out, Solodad?"

"Get high, dude, first thing."

"Aren't you afraid of getting violated and sent back to the joint?"

"Nah, the P.O. [parole officer] isn't going to test me on my first day out."

Solodad didn't *plan* on returning to prison on a violation, but with his dope-fiend mentality, he doesn't stand a chance of being successfully discharged from parole. Furthermore, he is not really worried about whether he returns to prison or not.

Any jointster will assert that he or she would rather be in the prison system than county jail. The reason is that the conditions are better in prisons. The transient ethos of a county jail population makes it difficult for inmates to improve conditions because they are often released or transferred before they can get anything done. County jails don't have the programs and resources that are available at prisons, which are designed for longer sentences.

One evening I was standing in line for commissary with a couple of my jailhouse friends, and this was the conversation that took place: Toe-tag explained: "You know, I wouldn't be here for robbin that liquor store if the damn clutch wasn't bad in that old Chevy of mine. Just as I was taking off, the motor died. I got it started, then it died again. That happened three times! By the time I made it to the corner, there were red lights everywhere."

"I hear ya brother, if my ole lady's mom wouldn't have turned me in, I wouldn't be here either," replied Straight Razor.

I understood those middle-aged bikers, because I have all too often placed the blame for *my* behavior outside of *me*. It would have been a waste of time for me to say, "Toe-tag, you wouldn't be here for robbin' a liquor store if you hadn't been robbin' a liquor store." It's strange, but that obvious statement does not occur to them, and it wouldn't have to me either. If someone would have suggested it, we would have considered it absurd.

My old friend, who is now doing life thrice, called me on the phone explaining—or whining (most drug addicts are chronic whiners), that he'd been arrested for something he didn't do. He carried on for five minutes about the injustice of it all. The whole time he was ranting on, I thought about the thousands of burglaries he had gotten away with. Finally, I asked: "Why are you so outraged about this?"

"Johnny, I didn't do it! God Damn them! The bastards are trying to frame me."

I then asked calmly "What about all those burglaries you've gotten away with over the years?"

"What? don't get carried away, Johnny. The fact is, I didn't do it. This charge doesn't have anything to do with what I did before." He dismissed my question as being utterly ridiculous.

Jointsters don't think like normal people. They can justify anything. I used to say that my crimes were victimless crimes because I didn't hurt anyone but myself by getting arrested for substance related offenses. I would have had an automated response if someone would have asked about the harm I was doing to my family, or the harm I could do while driving under the influence, or the harm I was doing to employers by stealing from them (hell, they could afford it).

When I was a bartender, I was in the bar on my night off. A couple guys asked if I could get them a quarter gram of speed. I said no. Later they asked me again, and again I said no. However, when they asked

me again around one o'clock, I knew someone in the bar that had
some—so I got the drugs for them. They were under cover policemen.
I fought the sales charge in a jury trial and lost. I took it all the way
through the court of appeals, and lost that too. *I was entrapped. It was
not my fault. They were picking on me.* The truth is, if I had not sold
drugs, I would not have gone to prison for selling drugs. However, I
was not at all capable of seeing it that way.

Unconsciously, many jointsters (mostly the ones who have gotten
used to doing time) are uncomfortable with the responsibility of living
in the free world. They break the law not only because they are angry,
bored, or need money, but because they are irresponsible, and they
don't want to take the time to work or do the things that aren't for
selfish purposes. Most jointsters are selfish and egocentric, and often
unhappy. Their unhappiness is not a cause but a companion to their
being irresponsible. The streets can be a frightening and depressing
place to be, because to many jointsters, being responsible and
accountable are alien concepts. An extreme and pathetic example is in
the movie *The Shawshank Redemption*, where actor James Whitmore's
character kills himself after being forced onto the streets against his will.

If we have no opportunity to be responsible inside the walls, why
should we become responsible outside of them? As I walked around the
yard, I could see the comfort zone that many of the inmates were
in—they seemed relaxed and at home. Their jovial camaraderie, "Hey,
home-boy, what it be like?" would give most observers the impression
that they are comfortable where they're at. Of course, the human
condition can get used to anything, and it is all too visible there. When
I see these jointsters on the street, they usually do *not* have the
appearance of being in a comfort zone—that relaxed, at-home look.
They seem a little more on edge. They appear more serious. For good
reason: They have much more to be serious and on edge about.
Everything is not provided for them the way it is in the joint. Thus, the
puer archetype somewhat diminishes through prison indoctrination, as
the criminalized drug addict starts personifying the trickster archetype
more.

Prior to the 1960s, the vast majority of convicts were in prison for
committing crimes. Not that many of them were committing crimes for
drugs or because they were under the influence of drugs. Times have
changed.

In Greek mythology, Hermes (the classical trickster) was known as
the messenger of the gods: in other words, mythologically, he connects
the gods and goddesses to each other and to man. Jointsters are

messengers too. As messengers they are trend setters. Prison yards are where many trends or fads originate, then they are introduced into society upon release dates or during visits. I remember seeing African Americans walking around the yard with their pants down low and their underwear showing. This is a common scene today. Ironically, back in the fifties we used to wear our levis down low too, but we didn't expose our underwear. Actually, we were worse. We exposed the cracks of our asses. Many expressions are also born in the joint, such as *home boy, it's all good,* or *dog* (short for road dog).

I have described the connection between addicts and their criminalization, but what makes these people tricksters? Weren't the prison populations prior to the 1960s also tricksters? Yes, but the astronomical number of jointsters housed in prisons today for drugs and drug-related offenses, makes a study like this valuable because we can identify inmates now as embodying archetypes, instead of just being convict scumbag sewer rats.

Carl Jung (1959) said that "the trickster is both subhuman and superhuman, a bestial and divine being, whose chief and most alarming characteristic is his unconsciousness." To say the least, addicts, especially after they have become criminalized, can be quite unconscious. Jung continued by saying that "because of it [the trickster's unconsciousness] he is deserted by his (evidently human) companions, which seems to indicate that he has fallen below their level of consciousness" (p. 263).

This quote by Jung calls to mind a situation among addicts when their friends desert them. An addict is capable of stealing another addict's dope, and then helping him look for it. Of course this scandalous behavior will cause the other addict to seek revenge or at least to abandon the relationship if he finds out about it.

When describing the trickster, Jung said, "He is so unconscious of himself that his body is not a unity, and his two hands fight each other" (p. 263). Criminalized drug addicts often exemplify the old saying about the left hand not knowing what the right hand is doing. Psychologically analogous to this idea is how most addicts expect to spend time in jails periodically—"that's just the way it is," they say. Or, they consider doing time in jail as dues paid to live the lifestyle they live, which was my attitude exactly. Yet, they will turn around and say that they are never going back to prison, that they're going to clean up and settle down with a nice woman, and "stop all this bullshit." Rarely they do, but most of the time they don't. Their left hand says they will and they're right hand says they won't.

Another example is how on the one hand the addict continually flirts with death; but on the other hand he has a high motivation to live. The irresponsible lifestyle he lives is what he considers 'living'. But what is not really considered to be 'living' to the joinster, is being stuck working a nine-to-five job, married to the same woman forever, and living in that stupid little house with the white picket fence. But the male drug addict is always "going to clean up, settle down and hook up with a nice woman, and stop all this bullshit." Most of us know which side wins. They continue to use, and they go to jail or prison, and they continue to use, and they go to jail or prison. Sometimes they also end up in mental institutions, homeless, or dead. Some aspects of the character of joinsters are often difficult for anyone to understand.

Wills & Carona (2000) describe a couple's despair:

> Nancy was forty-one. She'd been using drugs, on and off, for twenty-seven years. She seemed hopeless, doomed to die from a habit she couldn't break—though all along a single refrain ran through her mind: I can quit any time I want (p. 40).

Once this type of thinking is entrenched and bouts with the law are commonplace—whether it's DUIs or possession charges or anything linked to the use of chemical substances (felony or misdemeanor)—then they are hope-to-die dope fiends—drug-addicted jointsters who seems to defy *understanding*. *Understanding* the *puerile* trickster is also to recognize how creative they can be. Consider the creativity in the following story.

John, a meth addict, was attracted to Sagus' wife and took the opportunity to look down her blouse when Sagus wasn't looking. Sagus' wife asked, "Do you see something you like?" Surprised by her boldness, John admitted that he did. She said, "well, you can have it for $200." After thinking about it for about a millisecond, John agreed. She told him to be at her house around 2pm Friday.

John showed up at the house on Friday at 2pm sharp, paid the $200, had his way with Sagus' wife, and then hurried away.

As usual, Sagus came home from work at 6pm and upon entering the house asked his wife: "Did John come by the house this afternoon?" With a lump in her throat, she answered, "Why yes, he did." Her heart skipped a beat when Sagus asked: "And did he give you $200?" After mustering up her best poker face, she smiled and replied: "Yeah honey, wait a minute and I'll get it for you." Sagus, with a satisfied look on his face, said "good, I was hoping he did. John came by work this morning and borrowed $200 from me. He promised that he would stop by here on his way home and leave it with you." This is classic dope-fiend behavior—a classic trickster move, and wickedly creative.

Referring to the Zande trickster Ture of South Africa, Hynes and Doty (1997) suggest;

> We ought not to exclude entirely the possibility that such figures may voice anti-social feelings, insofar as the trickster often represents the obverse of restrictive order, but we must remember that tricksters or cultural clown-figures are not, as they would be considered in our culture, individually motivated deviants, but socially sanctioned performers (p. 7).

Yes, there are different types of people personifying the trickster archetype, even now in contemporary society, but we're focusing on the trickster archetype personified by criminalized addicts. There's irony in one of the ways the trickster archetype manifests in women with the pejorative reference to them as turning tricks. So, with women we have *puella* and the trickstress.

Not only does "every generation occupy itself with interpreting trickster anew," as Paul Radin (1972) reminds us, but tricksters are also interpreted differently in different cultures. For example, "in the Winnebago trickster cycle, trickster's sexual exploits are equally funny but not thought of as deviant. In a classic tale, Trickster came to a lake. On the opposite side he saw a number of women swimming, the chief's daughter and her friends. 'Now,' exclaimed Trickster, 'is the opportune time: Now I am going to have intercourse.' He then took his penis out of the box he had it coiled up in and said: 'My younger brother [speaking to his penis], you are going after the chief's daughter. Pass her friends, but see that you lodge squarely in the chief's daughter.' After a couple of failed attempts, he again sent his penis across the lake. The chief's daughter was the last one out of the water and could not get away, so the penis lodged squarely in her" (p. 19).

Joinsters too are horn dogs. Many go through women as fast as they do their drug stash. Remember, the negative pole of the *puer* is characterized by a poor adjustment to daily demands, a failure to set realistic goals and to make lasting achievements in accord with these goals, and a habit of intense and short-term relationships with women. As we can see, often the negative *puer* is commensurate with the jointster's trickster proclivities.

CHAPTER 5

IN THE WORDS OF JOINTSTERS
AS AUTHORS

To contribute more to an *understanding of the lived experiences* of criminalized drug addicts, let's consider what some of them have to say as authors about their experiences in and out of jails and prisons. Leder (2000), offers a compilation of reflections and dialogue between inmates incarcerated in Baltimore, Maryland. They ruminate about their lives and imprisonment. They discuss their thinking and the similarities between the inside and outside concerning lifestyle, coping mechanisms, recidivism, drug use, and their childhoods. One of the inmates, Tray, reflecting on his childhood in a dialogue group, shared:

> But sometimes memories can become real depressing. Me and John'll be talking and I'll tell him the first time I ever wanted to sell drugs. I was going into the seventh grade and I'd gotten fashion conscious. A dude gave me a job holding narcotics. I can remember sitting back there in the alley holding the stash for fifty dollars a night so I could save up for a slick wardrobe to start junior high (p. 89).

Whereas physical appearance isn't always as important to addicts as Tray's, their *image*—how they're seen by others, usually is. Consider what Donald had to say about image:

> I was having problems holding up my image in prison. I was in the shower and this other guy was trying to get past. I didn't want him to go behind me—you know what I mean—but he was trying to. So I popped him. But I was at a disadvantage of being naked and he got the best of me. He won the fight.

> Anyway, we made arrangements to meet at the gym an hour later so we could really fight. But someone stopped me at the door and said, "Look, that guy's a fool, but I thought you were a thinking guy." So he made me stop and think, and I didn't do anything (p. 186).

I realize that people from all walks of life do similar things for the sake of their image, but it is more pronounced with addicts. Many of us, for example, sport various types of facial hair and tatoos well into recovery. If not consciously, most of us are unconsciously wearing it as an insecure form of protection—a statement or signature—an image. Again, we bring some of the strangest things for the strangest reasons into recovery with us. Some of these anomalous things stay with us for the rest of our lives. Fortunately, we can shave off the facial hair and wear long-sleeved shirts if we need to change our image to present ourselves to potential employers, business contacts, or who or whatever. I have a friend whose arms, chest and back are covered with tatoos, and in meetings in the summertime he wears sling shot shirts. Most of those tattoos were put on *after* he got clean and sober. This really isn't unusual, it's a persona (which is another Jungian archetype, by the way).

Chevigny (1999) agrees:

> New inmates must learn how to recognize and respond to prison games if they are to navigate a course among treacherous allies or protectors and outright predators. This means adopting, or simulating, an appropriate role. In one way or another, all prisoners become players. For some, "doing time" and playing games are one (p. 129).

The criminalized drug addicted trickster has always been characterized as a *con* man (indicative of both *con*-vict and *con*-fidence man), and the personas he adopts has a broad range from the wiles of the prison yard to manipulation in the work force after he's released.

Again in Chevigny, Victor's story describes the manipulative mind-set of the jointster:

> In prison the tests were given so irrelevantly, inmates tended to see their results only as a tool of manipulation. Under this assumption, many men had developed theories on how to answer the test questions. Some felt it was best to copy from the brightest men in order to improve their chances at getting a clerk's job over kitchen or laundry duty. Others felt they

should give lunatic answers so they could be medically released from work altogether. Still others gave no answers at all and faked illiteracy, reasoning that they could enroll in school and appear to do extremely well, thereby fooling the parole board into believing they had worked hard to make a positive change in their lives. All these connivances were based on the inmates' understanding that they were being conned as much as they were doing the conning. They believed that the tests were used by the administrators just to maintain the semblance of educational purpose at best and at worst to harvest information from them that would some day be used against them—for example, in job placement or for parole eligibility (p. 17).

Turning to the topic of drugs, Scott wrote in Chevigny:

Though Hodgson blamed Strazinski for my stretch in the hole a month ago, I'd gotten myself in the jam. It began the day Cassidy, the aspiring vegetable—who'd huff dry cleaning solvent if it was the only way to get high—stalked into my cell and pulled out a joint the size of his finger. "You want to burn this with me, just say the word," he said, tossing a book of matches down onto the table like a dare. Cassidy's the kind of refugee who ambles through life like everything's casual, drifting in unannounced at the oddest moments to flash enough dope to get us both an extra year as if it were a candy bar (p. 61).

Also, Franklin (1998) quotes Malcolm X:

With some money sent by Ella, I was finally able to buy stuff for better highs from guards in the prison. I got reefers, Nembutal, and benzedrine. Smuggling to prisoners was the guards' sideline; every prison's inmates know that's how guards make most of their living (p. 150).

Shewan and Davies (2000) elaborate about drugs in prison: "In the eyes of many, acknowledging that drug use is a reality in prisons, would be to acknowledge that prison authorities have failed. And doesn't this mean that the government is basically admitting defeat—saying it can't control illegal drug use in prisons" (p. 17).

According to the December 2007 issue of *Prison Legal News*;

In January 2007, in Kern county California, Jail guards Donal
Lungren and Patrick Holloway were charged with selling and
possessing marijuana. Guard Josh Bankston was charged
with felony cocaine possession. The drugs were seized in the
guards's homes and vehicles. Also, on 15 October 2007,
Anthony Erodici, a state prison guard for 13 years, was
sentenced to 12 years in federal prison for cocaine trafficking.
At his sentencing Erodici claimed he became involved in drug
trafficking to feed his own addiction to cocaine (p. 42).

This apparently uncontrollable pandemic isn't just in the United
Stares—it's a major issue world wide.

Eight people in Pennsylvania, including four prison guards were
indicted for smuggling drugs and other contraband into the institution.
According to Fuocco (2006), grand jury documents reported "scenes of
drug dealing and double-dealing, secret codes and sexual favors,
payoffs and paybacks, intrigue and ingenuity, all swirling around
criminals and corrections officers acting in concert."

Chevigny (1999) also informs us that "the war on drugs is a
miserable failure because it has not stopped drug use in this country. It's
a great success [for prisons] because it's the best economic boom we've
ever seen" (p. xvi). Chevigny continues: "The prison-building boom,
the growing privatization of prisons, and private industry's use of
prison labor have so transformed the nation's economy that it seems
harder than ever to reverse the trend" (p. xvii).

Suzan Still (2002), who is an educator for the California
Department of Corrections, writes about the prison-building boom and
prison labor from a different perspective:

Unless we *free* citizens speak out and persist in seeing justice
done, we will find the institutionalization of slavery becoming
so embedded in the economic structure of this nation, that it
will seem impossible to maintain the economy without it. It will
become ineradicable. (p. 332)

The above quote is referring to big business—that of the prison
industrial complex. Still continues:

Prison industries showed a 40-billion dollar profit last year
[2001], yet inmates at our prisons are paid between 6 and 65
cents an hour. They have no benefits, no union, and no
vacations. Their work hours are not necessarily limited to 8
per day, nor are they compensated for overtime or hazardous
duty (p. 331).

Whereas I am not in favor of pampering inmates who deserve to be incarcerated, I don't see a separation of drug offenders and violent crime offenders happening anytime soon, or at all for that matter. Shouldn't prison be a deterrent to crime, rather than a day care center and a school of crime?

Donziger (1996) says that "more than 1.5 million Americans are behind bars (p. 33), and "five million Americans are under correctional supervision, and over 11 million people are admitted to locked facilities" (p. 34). And most staggering of all is that there are "fifty million criminal records" (p. 36). In no other country are there as many people locked up as there are in the United States, and only in Texas are there more locked up than in California.

Evans (2001) has given prisoners the chance to communicate things about themselves: Here is an excerpt from the foreword by Jimmy Santiago Baca:

> When I started reading *Undoing Time*, a con named Vincent came to mind. I'd helped him parole out: got him a job, his book published, paid for his literary readings, an apartment, and a car. Six months later, he relapsed into heroin and cocaine and went on a robbing spree (2001, p. ix).

Vincent could be the poster boy for the typical jointster. Given that this was all the author wrote concerning this con, we can only speculate about why he relapsed. The idea of relapse, in an effort to *understand* this population, is the rule rather than the exception. Taken from Evans (2001), Charles tells how..

> Years ago, after my parents split up, my old man took me to Long Beach, California with him, where we lived in an apartment over a bar. He had gotten out of jail and discovered my mom had been seeing another guy. So he took us kids. My older brother and sister were eventually sent to live with my dad's brother in Michigan, but I stayed with my father. I didn't mind. I loved my father very much. Dad was a bull of a man but very intelligent and loving. He was also an alcoholic. Cirrhosis killed him at forty-three. I was ten or eleven at the time and began to roam the streets a little at night. Me and my buddies would throw eggs at cars, shoot out porch lights with sling shots, or steal cans of whipped cream from grocery stores and gorge ourselves. When I'd get home from school, my dad would usually be at the bar downstairs, and there'd be two or three dollars on the table for me to buy my super with.

> Sometimes I'd go down to the bar and eat Slim Jims and play
> the electronic shuffleboard or bowling game. All the barflies
> would pinch my cheek and tell dad how awfully cute I was (p.
> 23).

When I read this, I couldn't help but think about my mom's
alcoholism, and me and my buddies' malicious mischief when I was a
youngster. Could these similarities between Charles and I have
predisposed us both to the lifestyle of criminalized drug addicts? Of
course it did, that's why young kids shouldn't be left to their own
devices, especially before, during, and after the pubescence years.

In Evans' Kevin writes;

> As I approached my eleventh birthday, I thought without a
> doubt that I was now grown. No one could tell me anything. I
> had developed a reputation as a fighter. My older brother and
> I were constant combatants; I had hit him with things and sent
> him to the hospital for stitches at least three times. Two or
> three days a week, he and I would be costars of the knock-
> down-drag-out neighborhood fight. I refused to let him think
> that he could dominate me. I had a fierce "little man" complex
> and was willing to meet any challenge if I thought someone
> was trying to slight me in any way. During that year, I became
> an ace pocketbook snatcher and could break into vending
> machines, pay phones, pinball machines—anything. I also
> became a dope fiend.

Wow! This guy must have been predisposed when he was much
younger, which isn't at all unusual. One of my friends was shooting
heroin when he was eleven years old, and that was back in the '50s, so
it isn't surprising that he died of an overdose when he was in his 30s.
Actually, it's probably a wonder that he lived that long. Melvin was the
type of junky that got as close as he could to death when he'd fix, then
nod off with cigarettes burning in his hand. As you might guess, he
burned to death in the trailer he was living in during one of his nods.

Edward Bunker (2000), actor, screenwriter, and author, has
epitomized the life of a jointster in his autobiography. Consistent with
much of the literature concerning drug addicts, Bunker says the same
about criminals: "If anything is true in a young criminal's mind, it is the
need for immediate satisfaction. Truly the place is here and the time is
now. Delayed gratification is contrary to his nature" (p. 92).

In another research project, I interviewed police officers, probation
officers, and prison guards. In this study one of the police officers made

the following statement: "I find that most of the people I deal with are only interested in the immediate time—the now. They can't see beyond the present, such as controlling anger, getting drugs or alcohol or money. Also, a difference in values, such as working for what you want, going to school, concerns for family; values of work, honesty, and a spiritual path." When I think about my years as a criminalized drug addict, I realize that I didn't want everything *now!* I wanted it *yesterday!*

William S. Burroughs (1977) was one of those tricksters who came from an upper-class background, studied at Harvard, became a heroin addict, then wrote a memoir entitled *Junky*. Later, after writing more than ten books, he also became an actor and director. Like Edward Bunker, he probably would have had little professional success had he not been addicted to heroin for so many years. This heroin addict, however, didn't stop being a trickster when he stopped using heroin, he just directed his trickster energy to a more productive lifestyle.

William S. Burroughs accidentally shot and killed his wife in front of their 4-year-old son, William S. Burroughs Jr. For 10 years after that, Burroughs Jr. only saw his father a few times, and they didn't spend much time together after that either. However, the lives of these father and son addicts ran a similar course up to a point.

In 1970, William S. Burroughs Jr. wrote *Speed*—the first of three books depicting his life as an amphetamine addict in New York's lower east side. At 34 years old, Burroughs Jr. died of liver failure due to alcoholism. But, it wasn't tricksterism that killed Burroughs Jr.—alcoholism did. Heroin addiction didn't cause the success of Burroughs Sr.—but tricksterism did. Like all archetypes, the trickster is a bi-polar phenomenon whose journey through life must be considered in ways that doesn't pigeonhole the jointster to the years when he was feeding his drug habit. Some of us do change.

Part of the *understanding* of these people is to realize that often what's under the veneer of who or what they're presenting (an image or a persona), is quite possibly another Edgar Alan Poe, Carl Jung, or Vincent van Gogh. But first they need to clean up and put an end to being thought of, and thinking of themselves as scumbag sewer rats.

CHAPTER 6

SCUMBAG SEWER RATS

omewhere around 1986 I had to visit my probation officer after having missed an appointment, so I asked my 18-year-old daughter to come with me. My thinking was—my inner trickster, that is—if he met this beautiful young daughter of mine, it might be enough to keep him from violating my probation and sending me back to jail. I introduced them, and they said hi to each other, then we all just sat there looking at each other—not saying anything more. Then my probation officer asked Lynda a question: "Did you know that your dad is a junky—a dirty scumbag sewer rat?"

My daughter looked at him gloweringly, holding eye contact with him momentarily, then replied "that's your opinion, not mine." Well, the probation officer didn't lock me up, so perhaps my trick worked. I never forgot that moment though. And as we will see, this notion of 'scumbag' is a common theme not only amongst jointsters, but also amongst the general public.

Every jointster I interviewed used the word *scum* to describe themselves as drug addicts as viewed by others. This particular theme resonated with me because of my own experience with having been described by a probation officer as a *scumbag sewer rat*—a theme which was then adopted as the title of my doctoral dissertation on the trickster archetype in criminalized male drug addicts.

In describing the way others view drug addicts, Dasher said: "They think we're freaks, and I'm guilty of it, you know. I see the people that are going down the street going like this [flailing his arms] and I think, 'oh, that poor son of a bitch.' Then I think 'but by the grace of God, there go I.'" Dasher also used the words *pity* and *fear* to describe how average people feel about drug addicts.

Dancer said that they [society] "probably think we're *scum*. You know what I mean? And now I look at these guys and I'll see them walking down the street, I just can't even—it's just dirty, you know. It's just dirty to me now."

After asking Prancer how he thought normies would describe us, he replied: "We would be basically labeled as *scum*, not to be trusted, not to leave anything laying around of value, you know." A little later he gave this scenario: "If I went into a—say, a church meeting and there was a bunch of people that never even did dope and I went in there and gave them my life story about how drugs messed my life up, they'd be looking at me with horror and think of me as *scum*. They wouldn't be able to relate to it at all—they'd be instantly scared of me. They wouldn't have compassion like another dope fiend would."

Compassion? Or did he mean *understanding*? Jointsters live with a perpetual mistrust of their own ilk, but that isn't to be confused with a lack of respect or even love. This is where one of the problems hide from normal people. How can normal people respect someone they mistrust? They can't! It's not rational to do that. Even jointsters have a difficult time doing it. We would be hard-pressed to find a jointster who trusts and respects police officers—they just don't exist, so the word trust is often used with ambivalence. Can it be argued that police officers, probation and parole officers, and correctional officers *understand* jointsters? Perhaps sometimes—in a way, but that understanding doesn't likely include compassion, trust, respect or love.

Here's Vixen's response to the same question about how others view addicts: "Oh shit, they looked at us as the degenerates of the world, the lowlifes of the world, you know, *scum*, the stuff that comes from under the rocks. I mean, what did the cops tell you when they busted you? 'You piece of *scumbag* shit!'"

After agreeing that normies look at us "with disgust, suspicion, and mistrust," I found myself wondering if Comet would use the word *scum* when I ask him: "If you had one word to characterize what the average citizen thinks of us as a general group, what would it be? "*Scum*," he replied. It's a word that every addict is familiar with. Then Comet said something similar to my other participants: "I'm sober 19 years and when I see that behavior, the word comes out of my mouth 'a bunch of *scumbag* mother-fuckers."

Even recovered addicts fall into the same mind-set as normies when it comes to respect. Whereas there was a *respect* for their peers prior to recovery, much of it is lost when they get clean and sober; therefore, an *understanding of the lived experiences* of jointsters will often be fraught with mistrust and an ambiguous element of respect and disrespect. But what about love?

I have friends who I drank and used with from our high school days to the time I stopped using. We don't associate together anymore, but we're still friends—the ones that are still alive, that is. I loved my friends then and I still do, including Jack—the one who is doing three life sentences for something he shouldn't even be doing one life sentence for. I cry at their funerals and I empathize with their families. Attempting to get the family members of jointsters to *understand* their natural, archetypal inclinations, proves to be fraught with difficulty. The emotional damage done by their jointster family members cannot seem to be bridged with an understanding that will give them the peace of mind they're looking for. They want their jointsters to get normal and act right. With an overwhelming majority of them, it's never going to happen, yet they will most always continue to enable them.

Kipnis (1991) reminds us that street drugs are expensive as well as illegal, so self-medicating men are much more likely to be arrested for crimes of social deviance. They often wind up in jails and prisons instead of treatment centers. Roughly ninety percent of all the inmates in the nation are male, and a substantial number of their crimes are either substance related or committed while under the influence (p. 275).

As I stated in Chapter One, personal experience is a valid reference tool. Qualitative researchers insist that qualitative methods are more appropriate than quantitative methods, because it allows for subjective knowledge. Phenomenological research is a qualitative research method often used in depth psychology that utilizes the interview process. Artistic research is also a qualitative method, which can include comedy skits and other types of acting, or it can include story. I have combined the phenomenological interview with the artistic element of story. This is called creative nonfiction.

Whereas the idiom *cattle rustling* is known in many jointster circles, it's not a phrase that's known by most people, at least not in the context in which many jointsters use it. Prancer was the cattle rustler out of those I interviewed. The vignettes that follow illustrate the life-like scenarios of cattle rustling, the cigarette and auto parts hustles, and other more conventional crimes.

Scumbag and his three road dogs, Poke, Jimbo, and Herby, met at Von's supermarket about noon. They agreed that if during the caper they got separated, they would meet later at Scumbag's house. They all lived in Riverside, California, and they would venture to surrounding communities to rustle cattle.

Each of them entered Vons except Herby, he remained in

Scumbag's pickup truck with the motor running, not far from the store's entrance. Herby was a weasel-looking little guy—the type who reminded people of a child molester or a sex pervert, which is why his buddies didn't want him going into the stores—his shady appearance was considered a liability.

These modern-day cattle rustlers entered the store separately so that they wouldn't draw attention. Once in the store, Scumbag accumulated several items before he found his way back to the meat section where he would load his basket with cattle—filet mignon, New York strip steaks, Chateaubriand, and flank steaks.

Scumbag's pain-*steaking* professionalism kept him shopping at a pace that wouldn't be likely to attract attention. When he got what he wanted, he positioned himself in an opportunistic location in the store near the exit, pulled a plastic bag out of his pocket and filled it with cattle from the grocery basket, then casually walked outside.

Herby was behind the wheel and ready to go. When it was obvious that no one was coming after him, Scumbag went to the bed of his truck and started putting the meat into an ice chest. Then, Scumbag and Herby waited in the cab for the next rustler to exit the store.

About 5 minutes later, Poke came walking out, and Herby was again ready for a quick getaway. Poke was a lanky six feet tall who had two speeds—slow and slower, so Herby had to be especially ready to pick him up if someone came after him. Fortunately, Poke made it, and he placed the meats in the ice chest and hopped into the bed of the truck. By the time Poke was done doing that, Jimbo exited the store—also without incident, so Jimbo jumped in the back with Poke and Herby drove slowly out of the parking lot.

Jimbo was the rowdy one of the team, and he talked too much. Already a three-time loser and on parole, one would think he would not want to go back to prison, but doing time was not a deterrent to crime for him. His motto was "don't do the crime if you can't do the time."

The cattle rustlers then made stops at various bars and restaurants where they sold their booty for half price to the patrons who were ready for a bargain. Once they off'd all the meat, the cattle rustlers pooled their money and sent Herby to score some dope. Herby was in the best standing with the heroin dealer at the time. An hour later, they were all at Scumbag's place adding more tracks on their arms and talking about the good ole days.

"Hey Poke," said Scumbag, "remember when we first started hustling the supermarkets?

"Yeah man, the cigarette hustle. We can't do it anymore because cigarettes are locked up now."

"Hey, I used to do that over in the Valley back in the 60s," chimed in Jimbo, "smokes were around ten bucks a carton and were out in the open where you could just stick 'em into a shoppin basket."

"That's right, and eleven of them would fit in a paper bag perfectly," added Poke.

"I was like 16 when I started, that was before I could grow a beard and before I had tatoos," continued Scumbag as he rubbed his nose and put out a cigarette.

"Yeah, and we didn't have to wear long-sleeved shirts back then either," commented Herby as he too scratched his nose. Among other quirks, people under the influence of opiates are continually scratching their noses because of the sensitivity of the blood vessels so close to the skin inside the nose. Most junkies avoid doing it as much as possible in public.

Scumbag and Poke had done the cigarette hustle similar to the way they did cattle rustling. Poke would traverse the supermarket, filling up the shopping cart with such things as dog food and charcoal. He'd go to where the smokes were and put eleven cartons in the basket. A little later Scumbag would come in with a paper bag folded up nice and neat and stuffed into his pants. When Poke saw Scumbag coming toward him, he would abandon the cart, go out and start the car, and have it right outside the door with the motor running and ready to go. Scumbag would extract the cartons of cigarettes from the cart, then push it to the front of the store, abandon the cart, and walk out like he had a bag of groceries. He'd get in the idling car with Poke, and away they would go.

These guys carry on when they're together like a group of teenagers. Any way you look at them, they're still modern-day outlaws with a one-track mind—getting high. Using the same characters, here's Prancer's information about the auto parts hustle.

Scumbag, Jimbo, and Herby set out on their plan. They got into Herby's car and drove to the neighboring community of Moreno Valley. Parking a block away, they walked to a Chief's Auto Parts store. There were two young guys working the counter. As Scumbag and his partners watched through the windows of the store, they noticed that one of the clerks made a trip to the back room, probably checking on the availability of parts.

That's when Scumbag entered the store and started shopping around. Jimbo came in a couple minutes later, but had to wait until the remaining counter man finished with a customer. Then he approached and asked: "How's it going, partner? Say, I'm looking for a set of points for a 1972 El Camino." About the time the counter man started going through one of those big auto parts books on the counter, Scumbag started grabbing things like high-dollar cams, intake manifolds, and high-performance Edelbrock carburetors.

What the other counter person was doing would determine how soon Herby would enter the store. They had to keep both countermen busy, so Scumbag could get out of the store with all the merchandise. When the young parts man returned from the backroom, Herby came in and asked him for something he knew they wouldn't have: "Hey pal, I need a water pump for a 58 Chevy 283. Would you *please* check to see if by any chance you might have one?"

With the two counter men kept busy doing other things, plus keeping an eye on the sleazy looking Herby, Scumbag made it out of the store, walked around to the back, and pulled a heavy-duty trash bag out of his pocket and filled it up with the parts. By the time the store employees figured out what happened to them, Scumbag and his fellow hustlers were gone. Scumbag walked out of the store with a couple thousand dollars worth of performance parts. Later, they would sell their booty for half price to mechanics at automotive garages, car dealerships, and service stations.

The three of them met at Herby's car and went to Scumbag's place, where they stashed the parts. Now it was time to sell the meat they had gotten earlier. By the time they did that, it was dark, and time to go pick up Scumbag's truck if it was still there. It was. They removed the stolen license plates and replaced them with the ones that belonged on it; then Herby and Jimbo left in Herby's car, and Scumbag went home in his truck. Not all jointsters, by the way, take the time to be so careful about not getting caught. They're usually in too much of a hurry.

Again these escapades are interesting, and even entertaining, but they are still the escapades of jointsters that aren't to be trusted; however, that doesn't mean that everything they do is of a negative, illegal, or immoral nature. They are still human beings who are worthy of redemption should they ever stop using drugs and continue their search for wholeness by other means. Scumbag demonstrates what I mean.

When Scumbag walked into his place, his answering machine light was blinking. It was one of his ex-girlfriends.

"Scumbag, this is Jackie, please give me a call. I really need to talk to you."

He dialed the number and sat down on his chair next to the telephone.

"Hello."

"How ya doing, old girlfriend? Is your killer body still turning heads like it always has?"

"You're sweet, Scumbag, I don't care what everybody says about ya. Hey, my mom is really struggling right now, and I was wondering if you could do me a big favor."

"If I can. What is it?"

"My mom's car broke down. She called her mechanic to come and tell her what it would cost to fix, but she can't afford the parts. She needs a carburetor. If she doesn't get the car running she can't go to work and she'll lose her job."

"Jackie, you're in luck. If you'll bring over a pint of tequila, I'll furnish the pot. I have the very carburetor that fits your mom's car."

"Scumbag, are you propositioning me?"

"No, I just miss hangin out with ya. Come on over and get the carburetor. Your mom needs it, so you can have it."

Jackie came over and knocked on the door. "Thanks, for the carburetor, Scumbag, and for saving my Mom's job. I really appreciate it."

"I didn't steal that carburetor for your mom, you know. On my way out of a wrecking yard, it was just sitting there asking to be taken, and there wasn't anyone around."

"You stole it! My God, Scumbag, my mom can't be putting stolen merchandise on her car."

"Would I put your mom in a position to go to jail? C'mon, take the carburetor, it's used, and I guarantee there's no way to trace it."

"Are you sure?" Jackie asked with a distrustful look in her eye.

"I promise. If anything like that happens, I will let you hit me as hard as you can in the head with a hammer."

"Okay, but I doubt if I would take the chance if she didn't really need it bad."

"Do you remember that rowdy-looking biker dude, Hercules, that I used to boost with?"

"No, not really."

"Well, he was six feet four, 250 pounds, with tatoos all over his body, and he was the bully type. He used to use his size to get what he wanted. Anyway, one day me and him was out boosting car parts in garages and gas stations and we went into this little garage in San Bernardino."

"Is this going to be a long one, Scumbag?"

"No, it's a short one, and I have a good reason for telling it."

"Okay, but I can't stay much longer."

"Yeah, yeah. Anyway, when this mechanic wouldn't buy anything, Hercules didn't like it. Jackie, this little mechanic had a gimpy leg and big thick glasses. I couldn't believe it. Hercules started to push this poor little guy around, so I said, 'c'mon Herc, let em alone. He doesn't want to buy. Let's go.' Then Hercules said to me: 'Shut up you little scumbag, I'll take care of this.'"

"That bastard?"

"Jackie, I couldn't believe he said that to me, so I picked up a pipe wrench and hit 'em up side of the head with it. Anyway, I didn't connect very well, so now I've got this fuckin' monster coming after me. He hit me and I went sailing across the garage, landing on an old car seat that was sitting on the floor. Well, in schools of martial arts, they tell us not to use our talent unless we have to, because our bodies are considered deadly weapons, and we can go to jail.

"You don't know martial arts, Scumbag!" Jackie retorted and laughing at the same time.

"How do you know what I know?"

"Never mind, go on with your story," Jackie said rolling her eyes back.

"Well shit, I was committing a felony anyway, so I came flying off that old car seat and caught him with my foot, but a car was in the way and it didn't knock him down. So I got him to the ground with an y-pa-soi-nagi, then chopped him in the adams apple. As he was . . . "

"What are you laughing at?"

"Nothing, Scumbag. Hurry up, I've gotta go."

Anyway, as he was laying there gasping for air and squirming around, I told the mechanic to get out of there, call the police, and not come back till they got here."

"Wow, Scumbag. I'm really impressed. You actually placed that little man before your own needs. That's really gallant."

"I realize I am usually thought of as a despicable junky, but I've told you this because I really don't want you to worry about your mom getting in trouble for putting stolen property on her car. I just wouldn't put her at that kind of risk."

"Wow, Scumbag. I'm beginning to realize that you are like that Don Quixote guy in the *Man of La Mancha*."

"Yeah, I've always been one to protect the underdog."

Jackie nudges his shoulder with her forehead. "I wonder why that is."

"Probably because I'm an underdog."

Here we see the humanity that's not always apparent when we think of criminalized drug addicts, whether they're personifying archetypes or not. My purpose here is an *understanding of the lived experiences* of this population. Though many of them shouldn't be trusted, most of them are worthy of the redemption that, say, a psychopath is not.

Hyde (1998) says that "the trickster is given something valuable with a condition set on its use, time passes, and before too long trickster's hunger leads him to violate the condition" (p. 28). Criminalized drug addicts' voracious hunger often causes them to flirt with death, leading to an overdose, and violating the condition set on the use of their lives. I found this to be true with the jointsters I interviewed.

Dancer told me about his experience: "I woke up one time in the back of somebody's fucking yard and they were squirting me in the face with a water hose. Another time I woke up and somebody was trying to shove me into my truck and push my truck out of the yard so I wouldn't *die* in their yard, you know."

Like me, by this time the 34-year-old Dancer had been in and out of jails for many years. Obviously, drugs and crime has made a seasoned jointster out of him. And like von Franz says: "the whole psychology of the drug taker is connected with the idea of flirting with death, getting away from reality and its hardships" (p. 88). Their risk-taking behavior is unconscious, however. Whereas they won't just walk into heavy traffic unconcerned, they will inject substances into their arms without any knowledge of its contents or strength. Whereas they will drive a car cautiously to avoid police while they're under the influence, when they need a fix they'll drive like maniacs, subjecting themselves and others to grisly accidents. Their criminal activity becomes more pronounced. Rather than rustling cattle or hustling auto parts, many of them resort to burglary and robbery. We might think that these people are entering the mind-set of the psychopathic, but we must keep *malesuada fames* in mind—drugs are a form of hunger urging people to crime. Consider this story in the life of Scumbag.

Dealing drugs was as much a part of Scumbag's life as using them, but it was never enough—he put too much of the profits into his arm. He needed to supplement his income to pay the dealer to insure that he would continue to have more to sell. Therefore, he participated in any type of criminal activity that would enable him to meet his financial obligations and still sustain the devil-may-care lifestyle and addiction to which he'd become accustomed.

Scumbag came to a time of his life when he was using speed and associating with a much different class of drug addicts than heroin junkies. The heroin addict is often thought of as the epitome of drug addiction by virtue of the addictive properties of the drug, and the lengths they will go to to get it, but a speed addict is the epitome of depravity—going to any lengths to satisfy his hedonistic appetite, which is fueled by more of a psychological expediency than a physical addiction.

As previously demonstrated by the tall tales told by Scumbag and his buddies, addicts are some of the world's best story tellers. Many of their stories start out being true, but by the time they finish they will have blown them completely out of proportion to what really happened. And many of them don't need that element of truth for their tall tales. This is called confabulation in medical circles because when addicts are questioned in emergency rooms, they often fill gaps in their memory with fictions, which they often don't even realize are fictions.

Scumbag and Huck were hanging out at Huck's place in Hinkley, a little town about 12 miles north of Barstow—the same area where Erin Brockovich exposed Pacific Gas and Electric for poisoning the residents with toxic waste.

Huck was another hippie-looking type with long hair and a beard, and he'd rather ride a Harley Davidson than drive a car, even if it were in the middle of the winter. However, since Huck had become involved with meth, he couldn't afford a bike.

Sitting around Huck's house in Hinkley, Scumbag asked, "Did you know that if it wasn't for me, the Erin Brockovich movie wouldn't have been made?"

Huck just sat there looking at Scumbag like he didn't believe him.

"I ain't shittin ya, man. I was at some friends house when Erin was there. After listening to what she had to say, I asked her if she wanted to get into the Department of Water to go through their records."

"Her boobs got her in there," challenged Huck.

"Bullshit, that's how Hollywood portrayed it. They couldn't admit in a movie that she was in there all night without permission. That's against the law. Check it out, I told her that if she would be there around six in the evening, I would get her into the building."

"So you broke in and helped her go through records, I suppose?"

"No, I got the key from someone I know that works there. Then I had one made and gave the key back. I gave Erin the key I had made, and that's all there was to it. You see, that guy would have never let her in there because of her boobs. And he isn't the wimpy type little guy that they made him out to be in the movie."

"Okay, I'll buy that, but what did you get out of it."

"We spent the following night together in a motel."

"You liar," said Huck. "You're seven feet tall and bullet proof, and now you expect me to believe that you slept with Erin Brockovich."

"I don't care if you believe me or not, but I would sure like to have some of that money that came out of all that."

"Yeah, me too."

I'm using the rest of this vignette to illustrate what Prancer did in his addiction.

"Speaking of money, I know some people in L.A. who buy stolen cars," said Scumbag.

"Hey man, every day when I leave Debbie's house, I can't help but check out this bitchin Toyota four-wheeler, and . . ."

Cutting Huck off, Scumbag said, "Wait a minute, Dick Head. Debbie lives right next door to a cop, right?"

"So what?" countered Huck. "We could steal his car too. He has a nice Honda Prelude that should be worth a lot."

"Hmm, I started to call you a fuckin idiot, but that's really not a bad idea. I know that cop. He gave me a ticket once for a chickenshit open container. He was a complete ass hole about it, too. He ran a make on me, checked out my car thoroughly, shined his light in my eyes—he did everything he could trying to find something to bust me on. Fortunately, he couldn't arrest me for anything. Damn good thing too, because I had an eight ball of speed taped to the inside of my leg."

"Okay then, let's take his car. He has it comin," said Huck.

"Well, let's check the situation and see if we can find a time when nobody's home at either house."

"Yeah, Scumbag, we'll get both of em. That's a good idea. Damn, I'm smart!"

On the following Saturday night there was nobody home at either house. So with Huck carrying a satchel that contained the needed tools, they walked to where the two cars were parked in their respective driveways, then approached the Toyota 4x4.

"Huck, hand me the satchel."

The satchel contained a pair of pliers, flathead screwdriver, phillips screwdriver, some extra screws about two and a half inches long, and a five-pound dent puller; a device used by body shops for taking dents out of cars. Scumbag sat the satchel down and walked around the car.

"Hey, where you going? Let's get this done," nagged the impatient Huck.

Scumbag looked at him with contempt and said, "hey stupid,

what's the sense in breaking into a car if it's unlocked?"

"Oh yeah, I was gonna suggest that."

Scumbag shook his head, and then started checking doors. They were all locked, so he stuck the screwdriver in the keyhole and hit it really hard so the screwdriver was embedded in the lock. Then he pushed down and popped the lock mechanism open. He grabbed the dent puller and got into the car, screwed it into the ignition and slid it out. He pulled it out and took the flathead screwdriver and stuck it in there like a key and started it—all in about 2 minutes.

"Huck, take this Toyota to your place and park it behind the house, and I'll see you there shortly."

Scumbag then took the satchel to the cop's Honda Prelude in the driveway next door. The driver door wasn't locked, so all he had to do was repeat the process on the ignition switch without having to break in. He started it and in about 20 minutes he was at Huck's place in Hinkley parking next to the other stolen car.

They went inside the house, shot some meth, and started talking 90-miles-an-hour. Among other things, they talked about the trip they were going to take the following night. Once they made their plan, Scumbag said, "Hey, did I ever tell you about the time I stole the Chevy Blazer in Victorville?"

"I think so," Huck replied, not particularly wanting to hear another one of Scumbag's tall tales.

"Naw, I don't think I told ya. Hey, I don't want you thinking that stealing cars is always as easy as it was tonight."

"Hey, it isn't like I've never stole a car before."

"Yeah, whatever. Anyway, one day, just after I started a Chevy Blazer, I put it in gear and started driving away. About that time this man grabbed the outside door handle, and started yelling at me to stop, threatening to kill me if I didn't. I took off, but he hung onto the door handle as I was driving away, saying shit like 'I'll not only kill you, I'll kill your fucking mother and your kids and whoever they're with!'"

"No way!" said Huck. "Was he a nut case or what?"

"Yeah, he was, and I found out later he was one of those mafia guys. Anyway, the asshole hung on for dear life. Huck, I was dragging him down the street. He held on and wasn't going to let go for nothin, still yelling obscenities at me. I didn't know what the hell to do. Finally, I rolled down the window, and while trying to drive at the same time, I pried his fingers off the door handle, and I left him laying in the street. When I looked in the rear-view mirror, I saw him bounce a couple times before he stopped. I never did see him get up."

"God damn, Scumbag. It woulda been easier to just let him have the damn car and gotten the hell away from there."

"I couldn't do that, I had a heroin habit at the time."

This banter continued for hours, and it's up to whoever reads it to believe it or not. All these stories are based on truth, much like the claims of many Hollywood movies. But just like the movies, how can anyone really know about all the dialogue and the various things needed to provide storylines, continuity, and interest. That's why movies say *based* on a true story.

Meth being a drug that causes people to talk incessantly, addicts sometimes hang around for days putting nothing into their bodies but more meth. Early the following morning, Huck started nodding off. "Hey, what are you doing? You can't go to sleep," said Scumbag.

"I've been awake a lot longer than you. I need some sleep."

"Okay," said Scumbag. "You'll be sorry if I find the soul of man and a cure for aging while you're asleep." But the prospect of missing out didn't seem to worry Huck at all.

Later that day Scumbag called his car-connection in L.A. and made a deal to sell the stolen cars. That night these two wild-eyed speed freaks somehow made it to San Diego and back without getting arrested, getting $5,000 each for the stolen cars.

Scumbag and Huck took their respective shares and went their separate ways. After spending so much time together in one stretch, both of them needed to be in the company of other people. Speed freaks get on each other's nerves after a while. Of course their paths crossed at drug dealers' houses periodically, and sometimes they would get high together.

Scumbag had been dealing crystal meth that he'd bought with his share of the stolen car money, but as usual he was using more than he was selling. He needed to supplement his income again; therefore, it was time to get into his car and take a ride before he ran out of money and dope.

Scumbag's (actually Prancer's) practice of breaking and entering was not limited to vehicles. Burglary is a widespread source of income for addicts of all kinds. He did it in much the same way as he did cars, except he used a hammer along with a screwdriver.

Scumbag drove around many rural areas in the high desert—Lucerne Valley, Victor Valley, Hemet, Palm Springs, Barstow, Morongo Valley and more. He looked primarily for people on vacation, but people working night shifts would do. He always worked alone on burglary jobs.

On a moonless night, he found an ideal place. Driving up to the house and sitting in his car for about five minutes gave him time to scan the premises for people peeping out of windows or neighboring house lights going off and/or on.

He got out and yelled, "is anybody home!" He wanted to arouse dogs or whoever else that might not have heard him when he first pulled up. He went to the front door and stuck a big screwdriver in the little crease between the door and the door jamb, then hit it with the hammer. The lock mechanism popped out and then he opened the door with a screwdriver and walked in.

Sometimes he used a crowbar—sticking it in there and busting the whole lock and everything off. What always baffled Scumbag is how many people only lock the bottom lock, leaving the dead bolt unbolted. When the deadbolt was also locked, he had to invest a couple extra minutes of his time to get a bigger crowbar.

A couple of days after his last burglary, Scumbag was driving around Lucerne Valley looking for prospective burglary sites when the red lights of a police car pulled in behind him. He wasn't carrying any stolen property and didn't have any outstanding warrants at the time, so he pulled over rather than trying to make a getaway.

Unfortunately, Scumbag went to jail because of some fingerprints he left behind at a previous burglary. He didn't even try to fight it, knowing that he would have to stay in the county jail for as long as two years before his inevitable conviction and subsequent sentence to the state penitentiary.

He pleaded guilty and was sentenced to 3 years in the *California Department of Corrections*. The state prison at Jamestown, California had a strong work program, an effective pre-release program, and a Narcotics Anonymous program. Through Narcotics Anonymous, he entered the recovery process one more time.

Like most of his partners in crime, Scumbag was in and out of jails and prisons for most of his life. Prison was a home that he'd become accustomed to. Stealing becomes a trickster's way of life that John Fogerty captures in his song Vanz Kant Danz:

> Vanz can't dance, but he'll steal your money,
> Watch him or he'll rob you blind.
> You're watchin' 'em dance, not a care in the world;
> So Billy and Vanz get busy, they're makin' their move;
> The little pig knows what to do, he's silent and quick, like Oliver Twist;
> Before it's over, your pocket is clean,
> A four-legged thief paid a visit on you.

Laying on his bunk in his cell, his bunky Soledad, said, "hey Scum, I've had it with drugs. I'm sick and tired of being sick and tired. What are those meetings that you've been going to? Ya think they might help me?"

"If you are willing to do what it takes," replied Scumbag.

"What does it take?"

"Well, it takes *want* power. You've gotta *want* to be clean and sober more than you've ever wanted anything in your entire life. You have to go to 90 meetings in 90 days. You have to get a sponsor. You have to read the literature. You have to work the 12 steps. You have to be willing to turn your life over to a power greater than yourself. You have to . . .."

Soledad cut him off and said, "Hey wait a minute. I sure have to do a lot. I'm not sure I can do all of that."

"Then you don't want to clean up. If you really want it, you'll squat down like a duck and quack up and down main street if that's what it takes.

"I don't know about the squatting and quacking, but I wanna clean up, Scumbag. I'm really sick of all this. I've been doing it for too long, and I don't want to come back to places like this anymore.

Scumbag became Soledad's sponsor in Narcotics Anonymous while they were in the joint, and when Soledad was released from prison he was transformed, and never did another drug for the rest his life, not even aspirin.

Too bad Scumbag couldn't practice what he preached, because 30 days after his release he was back in the joint for a violation of parole. Scumbag was a typical jointster, but it's Soledad who was the exception to the rule.

CHAPTER 7

LEGACIES OF THE JOINTSTER
EVOLUTION OF THE CRIMINAL JUSTICE SYSTEM

The criminal has evolved historically, and this is how and when. Imagine a Neanderthal man named Moger leaving his cave to forage food for his family. Moger is responsible, the kind of man who stands on his own two bare feet and works hard hunting from dawn to dusk so his family can live in caveman comfort.

A few caves down the valley lives a neighbor named Cleb. Cleb is a shifty, lazy, deadbeat scumbag sewer rat—an irresponsible, beady-eyed creep who sleeps a lot, freeloads off the generosity of others, and is known to imbibe certain mind-altering herbs of the forest.

One day Moger is returning home to his cave, dragging a small saber-toothed tiger by the tail, when he notices that a large hunk of venison that he had hanging up to dry had disappeared. It doesn't take much for even the slow mind of a caveman like Moger to conclude that his no-good, irresponsible scumbag neighbor Cleb, has ripped him off again.

Moger picks up his club and stalks straight down the valley to Cleb's rundown, dilapidated cave and finds the full-bellied Cleb smacking and drooling and gnawing on Moger's hard-earned venison bone. Anger and revenge flood through Moger's prehistoric mind as he clubs the old junky over the cranium, knocking him senseless. Moger picks up what is left of his venison bone and strolls on home with a self-satisfied grin on his face. A wrong is made right and thus was the dawn of the criminal justice system.

Though such executions as that of Socrates in 399 BCE were carried out over the next millennium, it is not known when burning at the stake was first used. In Britain however, there is a recorded burning for heresy in 1222, when a deacon of the church was burnt at Oxford for embracing the Jewish faith so he could marry a Jew, and Joan of Arc was burned at the stake on 30 May 1431 in Rouen, France. From the Greek and Roman empires to the Inca civilization in Meso-America to 18th-century Europe, punishment by decapitation was viewed as a humane way of death—one often reserved for the elite of society. Unlike other methods, the lopping off of heads was decidedly quicker and less painful than, say, the horribly slow and agonizing demise that came with being impaled on a stick, burned at the stake, or drawn and quartered.

The recorded history of punishment began with torture and execution, often as public spectacles. For example, Foucault (1977) tells us that as late as 1757 a man was taken in a cart wearing nothing but a shirt, holding a torch of burning wax weighing two pounds; then after being placed on a scaffold, the flesh was torn from his breasts, arms, thighs and calves with red-hot pincers. His right hand burnt with sulpher, and on those places where the flesh was torn away, molten lead, boiling oil, and burning resin, was poured on. His body was drawn and quartered by four horses, and his limbs and body consumed by fire, and then his ashes were thrown to the winds. It makes one wonder, who would commit a crime back then knowing what would happen if he or she were caught?

As early as 1760, a hanging machine had been tried out in England. It was improved and finally adopted in 1783. The guillotine however, first used in March 1792, was the perfect vehicle for punishment. Death was reduced to a visible, but instantaneous event.

The roots of the word 'prison' comes from the term *prisune* from before 1112, which means confinement. *Prisune* was influenced by *pris*, which means taken or seized. From Latin *prehenso*—to lay hold of, clutch at. *Prysner*—one kept in prison—probably arrived somewhere between 1350 and 1375.

The earliest records of prisons, according to Morris and Rothman (1995), "are in Egypt and date from 2050 to 1786 BCE. The pharaohs acknowledged a sacred duty to preserve public order. On these principles, expressed in the concept of *maat* (justice or order), depended the equilibrium of the universe." Pharaohs and their servants could be neither arbitrary nor cruel, and Middle Kingdom pharaohs appear to have preferred public beatings and imprisonment to the death penalty. One of the most useful accounts of prisons in ancient Egypt is the passage in the Book of Genesis (39:20 and 40:5) describing the confinement of the Hebrew slave Joseph by the Egyptian royal official Potiphar.

The Assyrian empire (746 to 539 BCE) imprisoned smugglers,

thieves, deserters from royal service, and tax evaders. Skipping over some of the intermittent history, we go to "451 BCE, when the only instance of imprisonment occurs in the laws concerning debt. Debtors who could not or would not pay were to be held in private confinement by their creditors for sixty days and were to have their debts publicly announced on three successive market days, on the last of which they might be executed or sold into slavery outside the city" (p. 8, 9).

There is one more category of imprisonment during this period. The limitless powers of the male heads of Roman households included the right to maintain a domestic prison cell to discipline members of the household. This cell, the *ergastulum*, could be a work cell for recalcitrant or rebellious slaves or a place of confinement at the pleasure of the father for any family member for any infraction of the household discipline.

> In Rome, in 198 BCE, the consuls ordered the lower magistrates to double their prison precautions. Later, in 576 CE, Kings sometimes used monasteries as prisons for captured rebels, and by the thirteenth century some instances of monastic penitential imprisonment were designated by the formal term 'punishment' (p. 17).

"From the 1270s on, the number of prisons in England increased rapidly, and by 1520 there were 180 imprisonable offenses in the common law." (p. 31) The system of prisons that emerged from France however, lasted until the French revolution in 1789.

Between the years 1830 and 1848 public executions had almost entirely disappeared. It was in the 1830s that prisons were organized around principles of order and regularity and subseuently isolated each prisoner in a cell and enforced rules of total silence.

Public execution and various forms of punishment were the antecedents to the prison systems we're familiar with today. From the stake and public square, it spread by word of mouth— *verbodissemination*. For as long as criminals have been around in their various forms, the general public and popular media (especially prior to the 1960s) has pigeonholed a general criminal-type that includes descriptors such as 'gangster' 'psychopath' or 'ex-con'. These descriptors are not mutually exclusive stereotypically. Their peccant personalities are often described as hardened, violent, immoral, racist, devoid of compassion, destructive, and untrustworthy—hell kites.

Kipnis (1999) reports studies done by the Prison Activist Resource Center that lists the top ten reasons for Californians entering prison:

1. Possession of a controlled substance
2. Possession of a controlled substance for sale
3. Robbery
4. Sale of a controlled substance
5. Second-degree burglary
6. Assault with a deadly weapon
7. Driving under the influence
8. First-degree burglary
9. Petty theft with a prior conviction
10. Vehicle theft

Clearly, violent crime is practically absent (p. 176).

According to Kipnis, drug offenders represent sixty percent of federal prisoners and over one-third of state and county prisoners (p. 121). Storie (October/November 2007) explains that the National Institute on Drug Abuse (2002) figures show that 70-85 percent of California state inmates have substance abuse problems serious enough to warrant treatment (p. 4). Considering those percentages, let us examine the top ten reasons for Californians entering prison, which is likely to be similar in other parts of the country. Numbers one, two, four, and seven are directly substance-related. However, how many of the people incarcerated for numbers three, five, eight, and nine were getting money to support a habit or simply for the recreational use of drugs and/or alcohol?* And how many of 'number six" assaults (the only one involving destructive behavior) were committed while under the influence? That would be hard to determine, as would the correlation existing between number ten and substances.

Prior to the 1960s, the criminal archetype was synonymous with the convict stereotype. Since then, the convict started transforming into the inmate, which was the ending of the convict, but not the ending of the convict stereotype. And this is where a *hoc opus* arose—a symptomatic breakdown in our culture that occurred chiefly because of the consciousness created by the media. The preponderance of the prison population since the 1960s are the chemically dependent *inmates*—not the stereotypical convicts—a media image. The inmate is still viewed as the convict. This media image is a living myth, one that has influenced and even structured our culture. Campbell (1988) shares; "every mythology has grown up in a certain society in a bounded field.

---

* Among the 5.3 million convicted offenders under the jurisdiction of corrections agencies in 1996, nearly 2 million, or about 36%, were estimated to have been drinking at the time of the offense (Bureau of Justice Statistics Home Page).

Then they come into collision and relationship, and they amalgamate, and you get a more complex mythology" (p. 22). Let us consider another *symptom* contributing to a breakdown in our culture.

Is prison a deterrent to crime? Judging by the recidivism rates, no. Many see recidivism as the result of a perversion of the formal aims of imprisonment. What are the formal aims of imprisonment? Foucault (1977) says that "formal punishment started as revenge, then shifted to the defense of society" (p. 90). We could easily argue that it has shifted back to a *lex talionis*—'an eye for an eye'— when considering such statements as "lock em up and throw away the key," or "he got exactly what he deserved," or when considering the war on crime, or the three strikes legislation. Revenge is, indeed, another *symptom*—a *schadenfreude*, further deteriorating our values toward fellow human beings.

Most people probably have a difficult time admitting that their idea of punishment is really revenge. Whatever their reasons for supporting punishment, they should probably consider what is going on *intra muros*—within the walls of our prisons, especially the ones I am familiar with—the federal prison system and the California Department of Corrections. Those who want revenge certainly would not want to continue to pay an astronomical amount of tax dollars to make sure the ciphers of such a netherworld are well taken care of; some might even say pampered. Not to mention the money spent interminably building prisons. In my 1995 magazine article entitled *Prison: The Day Care Center*, I share the nimiety of my prison experience by explaining that inmates are so well provided for, that prison isn't a deterrent to crime— at least as per the lower security yards in California; and that would be levels one and two.

Prior to emphasizing the benefits of a federal correctional institution in Pennsylvania, Worth (1995) explains that "with visitors, it's like a joke, to see how long before they compare this place to a college campus." Federal prisons have had the reputation as "resorts" or "country clubs" for a long time. It is my contention that prison systems—especially the ones just mentioned, are in many ways a major *symptom*atic breakdown of our culture. Of course the media image presented by motion pictures and television does not reflect these symptoms. What they do—since the 1960s that is—is perpetuate a stereotype of a criminal, not a drug addict.

Morris and Rothman (1995) offer one day in the life of #12345:

If you expect the usual prison tale of constant violence, brutal
guards, gang rapes, daily escape efforts, turmoil, and
fearsome adventures, you will be deeply disappointed. Prison
life is really nothing like what the press, television, and movies
suggest. It is not a daily round of threats, fights, plots, and
shanks (p. 203).

I am not suggesting that everything we see and read in the media is
inaccurate concerning the criminal element—some is; for example,
prison can definitely be a parlous environment—an Augean* stable,
with the nefarious lifers preying on the often pusillanimous fresh fish
of youth—*ovum lupo committere*, to entrust the sheep to the wolf. For
the most part however, our ocularcentrism has been developed and
indoctrinated by the power structure.

Where do the *puer* and trickster archetypes fit into this history, or
any history for that matter? Archetypes are timeless and universal. They
are in all cultures *ab ovo*—from the beginning, and *ad infinitum*—to
infinity.

DRUG HISTORY AND THE NUMINOSUM

Wanting to feel good is visceral. In whatever form we choose, whether
it be religious revivals, speaking in tongues, going on vision quests,
meditating, ejaculating or doing drugs—it can still be thought of as
numinous—a supernatural state. In one way or another, from time
immemorial drugs have played a role in religion. From the ancient
Mayans and African tribal beliefs to modern day Shamanism. Often, the
drugs used were seen as opening the gateway to the "spirit world" and
only spiritual leaders would use them on behalf of their people. Corbett
(1996) explains;

The imagery of the shaman's journey is fairly similar in its
themes in different parts of the world because the shaman
experiences directly those categories of the imagination
which are archetypal. To reach them, the shaman enters or
evokes the necessary state of consciousness through ritual,
or by means of the enactment of myth, which allows access
to the spirit world (the transpersonal levels of the
unconscious). Techniques such as fasting, drumming,
dancing or *hallucinogens* all produce intense affective
arousal, expansion of the spectrum of ordinary perception

* Augeas, the mythical king of Elis, kept great stables that held 3,000 oxen and had not been
cleaned for thirty years--until Hercules was assigned the job. Hercules accomplished this task
by causing two rivers to run through the stables.

and a submersion or suspension of consensual reality. Such altered consciousness is often necessary for the evocation of archetypal material (p. 125).

When we think of drugs however, we think of the illicit ones like cocaine, marijuana, meth, heroin and LSD,* but we overlook the seemingly insignificant and socially-acceptable licit drugs such as nicotine and caffeine. Plus I only mention passively the use of alcohol in Christian rituals such as the Eucharist. However, when a Christian drinks the blood of Christ, they do not do so to the extent of oblivion. Neither does the exploration with drugs on a Shamanic level lead to recreational euphoria. It's not like the societal disturbance we see with an alcoholic or heroin addict. It's the use of a drug for a constructive mental process. The difference being that in once case one often sets out to destroy the mind whereas the other sets out to educate it.

Our society is presently saturated with the often *puerile* overindulgence in chemical substances. Of course there is no shortage of *senex* overindulgence either. Yet, less than a hundred years ago people were drifting blissfully in the clouds of Morpheus. Morphine and laudanum† were highly recommended for many ailments, as was smoking tobacco. Today the drugs may be stronger and more destructive, but perhaps their abuse is in some way a form of spirituality; such as teenagers attempting to alleviate the boredom in a boring society not geared to nurture their individuality and accommodate their spiritual needs. Or, in the words of Weil (1972): the ubiquity of drug use is so striking that it must represent a basic human appetite. Weil also suggests that altering consciousness is innate. Perhaps the internal need to release inhibitions, be devious, act crazy, fight, gamble, chase women, lie, cheat, and steal is also an innate need to alter consciousness (p. 17). There are a litany of 12-step programs today offering recovery to a wide variety of compulsive behaviors—programs such as alcoholics anonymous, narcotics anonymous, overeater's anonymous, smokers anonymous, gamblers anonymous, sexaholics anonymous, debtors anonymous, and workaholics anonymous—just to name a select few.

---

* A quite different acronym for LSD is: pounds, shillings and pence, in the former English coinage. L = Libra (a pound); S = solidus (a shilling); d = dendrius (a penny). There is a humorous expression L.S.Deism, meaning 'worship of money' (*A Dictionary of Latin Words and Phrases*, p. 101).

† This name is said to be used by Paracelsus in other than the ordinary sense, and to signify a specific for fevers which was a compost of gold, corals, pearls, etc. Another writer says that it is a medicine beyond all praise, made out of two substances, than which nothing more excellent can be found in all the world, and whereby almost every disease is cured (*A Short Lexicon of Alchemy*).

With well over 50 'anonymous', and many other types of support groups without "anonymous" tagged onto it, that constitutes a considerably large population of *supposedly* sick people.

The use of opium goes back unofficially to the ancient cave dwellers of Moger and Cleb, who drew pictures of the poppy plant on the cave walls. Officially, according to a *Frontline* history on the Internet, it goes back to 3400 B.C.E. where it was cultivated in lower Mesopotamia. The Sumerians refer to it as Hul Gil, the 'joy plant'. The Sumerians would soon pass along the plant and its euphoric effects to the Assyrians. The art of poppy-culling would continue from the Assyrians to the Babylonians who in turn would pass their knowledge onto the Egyptians. In 460 B.C.E. Hippocrates, 'the father of medicine', dismisses the magical attributes of opium but acknowledges its usefulness as a narcotic and styptic in treating internal diseases—diseases of women and epidemics. By the 1300s opium disappeared for two hundred years from European historical records. It had become a taboo subject for those in circles of learning during the Holy Inquisition, then it resurfaced again in Portugal in the 1500s. In 1680, English apothecary Thomas Sydenham introduces Sydenham's Laudanum. Laudanum was a wildly popular drug during the Victorian era. It was an opium-based painkiller prescribed for everything from headaches to tuberculosis. Laudanum's biggest clam to fame however, was its use by the romantic poets. Many of the Pre-Raphaelites (among them Lord Byron, Shelly and others) were know to indulge.

Tussionex was my Laudanum. For eight and a half years I sustained a diurnal practice of writing and filling pharmaceutical prescriptions for it. Getting arrested by the police was nugatory—dues I had to pay for my addiction. During those parlous years I was arrested four times on felony charges, only being convicted twice on misdemeanors. What made Tussionex a schedule-three controlled substance was hydrocodone resin complex. Unlike the fugacious cocaine, it had a long duration—from eight to twelve hours (its formula has since been changed). I share the opinion with others that Tussionex was the most superior opiate drug; a virtual halcyon* of euphoria. The numinosum however, is not always upbeat and wonderful. There isn't anything spiritual about the often scabrous struggle to sustain an opiate

---

* According to Greek mythology, Alkyone, the daughter of the god of the winds, became so distraught when she learned that her husband had been killed in a ship wreck that she threw herself into the sea and was changed into a kingfisher. As a result, ancient Greeks called such birds "alkyon" or "halkyon." The legend also says that such birds built floating nests on the sea, where they so charmed the wind god that he created a period of unusual clamor that lasted until the birds' eggs hatched.

addiction, whether it's heroin from the drug dealer or pharmaceuticals from the pharmacy obtained by forged prescriptions.

The numinosum *can* be negative. When Corbett (1997) mentions Mark, Luke, Matt and Cor., when discussing celibacy, he mentioned that "the body and sexuality acted as a kind of negative numinosum" (p. 161). My body and Tussionex acted as a negative numinosum, in that I kept going back for more despite the problems that being a drug store bandit were causing me. Life on a daily basis was like being under the sword of Damocles, which makes the family of opiates the most opprobrious and addictive; hallucinogens however—especially peyote and mescaline, are thought of as the most mind-altering and spiritual.

Concerning the origin of religion—especially the ancient mystery cults—Wasson (1986) shares with us;

> In Antiquity people spoke of the Mystery of Eleusis, of the Orphic Mysteries, and of many others. These all concealed a secret, a 'Mystery'. But we can no longer use 'Mystery', which has latched on to itself other meanings, and many of us all know the uses and misuses of this word today. Moreover, we need a word that applies to the potions taken in the antique Mysteries, now that at last we are learning what they were. 'Hallucinogen' and 'psychedelic' have circulated comfortably among the Tim Learys and their ilk back in the 1960s, for the lack of a suitable word. Hallucinogen is patently a misnomer, as a lie is of the essence of 'hallucinogen', and 'psychedelic' as a barbarous formation. No one who respects the ancient Mystery of Eleusis, the Soma [mushroom]· of the Aryans, and the fungal and other potions of the American natives, no one who respects the English language, would consent to apply 'hallucinogen' to those plant substances. Antiquity remained silent on these plant substances, for they were never mentioned, except perhaps person to person in a low voice, by the light of a candle at night. Gordon Wasson and others formed a committee under the Chairmanship of Carl Ruck to devise a new word for the potions that held Antiquity in awe. After trying out a number of words they came up with *entheogen* "God generated within," not to replace the Mystery of the ancients, but to designate those plant substances that were and are at the very core of the Mysteries (p. 30).

John H. Laney (1972) quotes La Barre expressing the following anthropological opinion:

· The term Paracelsus used was Boletus. Bolitus is the same as Bolbiton, *i.e.*, the excrement of oxen (*A Short Lexicon of Alchemy*).

"Without a doubt [it is] the most widely prevalent present day [1947] religion among the Indians of the U.S. . . . the use of Peyote has spread from group to group until today it has assumed the proportions of a great intertribal religion" (p. 110). Laney continues; "the movement has been referred to variously as Peyotism, Peyote Cult or Sect, and Peyote Religion. The members themselves know it nominally as The American Church of North America. I prefer to call it the peyote movement because of its creatively dynamic character" (p. 110). "It has also been referred to as Father Peyote, Peyote Jesus, holy food, our brother, and medicine. ('Medicine' in the Indian sense, meaning a manna substance, is capable of curing the mind as well as the body)" .

The spiritual ambiance of the peyote movement wasn't necessarily an organized religion. "Owing probably to the strongly individual orientation of the members," says Laney (1972), "as well as to their interest in, and closeness to, the original religious experience, there is no theology in the movement, no officially formulated doctrine" (p. 112). Whereas I have not had personal experience with peyote, I have had considerable experience with LSD.

I spent roughly five years experimenting with psychedelic drugs—mostly LSD. I have fond memories of those years, without ever having had a bad trip. Was I a netherworld criminal who was in possession and under the influence of illegal drugs, or was I having spiritual experiences by means of nonordinary states of consciousness? According to state law, I was a firebrand—stirring up trouble and committing crimes. According to me, *then*, I was just getting high. According to me, *now*, I was experiencing the numinosum through nonordinary states of consciousness, as well as getting high. Today, I do not condone the recreational use of drugs. In fact, I advocate total abstinence, but I have to ask myself: do I regret the past? No. I believe I am who I am today because of how I lived my life—*quantum mutatus ab illo**—changed from the person you once were. Without those psychedelic experiences with LSD, I believe there would be a part of me missing—an asset, I might add, for in some ways I can still see through those entheogenic eyes. If one wants to experience the numinosum through nonordinary states of consciousness, heroin addiction is always an option. Not really, I'm joking, but there are better ways to do it. A more acceptable manner is psychiatrist Stanislav Grof's holotropic breathwork.

Grof (2000) shares;

---

* Aeneas sees the blood-bolstered ghost of his fellow Trojan Hector in a dream and exclaims over how unlike he now is to the Hector who came back from the battlefield clad in the armour of his enemy Achilles (*A Dictionary of Latin Words and Phrases*).

In the last twenty-five years, my wife Christina and I have
developed an approach to therapy and self-exploration that
we call 'holotropic breathwork.' It induces very powerful
holotropic states by a combination of very simple means—
accelerated breathing, evocative music, and a technique of
body work that helps to release residual bioenergetic and
emotional blocks. In its theory and practice, this method
brings together and integrates various elements from ancient
and aboriginal traditions, Eastern spiritual philosophies, and
Western depth psychology (p. 183).

Before holotropic breathwork, Grof and other physicians
discovered a number of therapeutic uses for LSD. Grof (2000) explains;

In the early 1960s, Eric Kast of the Chicago Medical School
studied the effects of various drugs on the experience of pain
in search of a good and reliable analgesic. During this study,
he became interested in LSD as a possible candidate. In a
paper published in 1963, Kast and Collins described the
results of a research project, in which the effects of LSD were
compared with two established potent narcotic drugs, the
opiates Dilaudid and Demerol. Statistical analysis of the
results showed that the analgesic effect of LSD was superior
to both opiates. (p. 250).

I don't recommend trying this. These researchers were doing this
under controlled conditions.

That was just one medical use for LSD. There are also psychotherapeutic uses. Grof continues:

The encouraging results of Kast and Collins's studies inspired
Sidney Cohen, a prominent Los Angeles psychiatrist, friend of
Aldous Huxley and one of the pioneers of psychedelic
research, to start a program of psychedelic therapy for
terminal cancer patients. Cohen confirmed Kast's findings
concerning the effect of LSD on severe pain and stressed the
importance of developing techniques that would alter the
experience of dying (Cohen 1965). His co-worker, Gary
Fisher, who continued these studies, emphasized the
important role that transcendental experiences play in the
treatment of the dying, whether these are spontaneous,
resulting from various spiritual practices, or induced by
psychedelic substances (p. 251).

In my case, during the time that I was experimenting with LSD, the term psychedelic was suitable. However, considering the numinous benefit of those experiences that I have now, I am inclined to use the term entheogen, depending on the context in which it's being used. Although I haven't found the term entheogen relegated to the coca plant in any of the literature, I think that it would be suitable prior to its synthesis.

At another web site, this one sponsored by *Narconon,* we can find cocaine history:

> Cocaine in its various forms is derived from the coca plant that is native to the high mountain ranges of South America. The coca leaves were used by natives of this region and acted upon the user as a stimulant. The stimulating effects of the drug increases breathing which increases oxygen intake. This afforded native laborers of the region the stamina to perform their duties in the thin air at high altitudes.

Whereas *Narconon* didn't provide any dates with the above description of the coca plant, it does with the chemical synthesizing of it. *Narconon* also shares that "Cocaine was first synthesized in 1855. It was not until 1880, however, that its effects were recognized by the medical world. The first recognized authority and advocate for this drug was world famous depth psychologist, Sigmund Freud. Early in his career, Freud broadly promoted cocaine as a safe and useful tonic that could cure depression and sexual impotence.* Cocaine got a further boost in acceptability when in 1886 John Pemberton included cocaine as the main ingredient in his new soft drink, Coca Cola. It was cocaine's euphoric and energizing effects on the consumer that was mostly responsible for skyrocketing Coca Cola into its place as the most popular soft drink in history. From the 1850's to the early 1900's, cocaine and opium laced elixirs, tonics, and wines were broadly used by people of all social classes. This is a fact that is for the most part hidden in American history. The truth is that at this time there was a large drug culture affecting a broad sector of American society. Other famous people that promoted the "miraculous" effects of cocaine elixirs were Thomas Edison and actress Sarah Bernhart. There is a longer list of historic figures that used cocaine and other drugs, but in the interest of brevity, I won't elaborate.

---

* To read more on Freud and his addiction to cocaine, go to my website @ www.ScumbagSewerRats.com and read my article, *Was Freud a Depraved, Drug Addicted Deviate?*

Laney (1972), referring to the peyote movement, says;

"in my experience, not only does a general lack of information
exists about this movement, but a quantity of dramatic
misinformation exists in its place; that it belongs somewhat to
the 'drug culture', that it is a decadent, deteriorating religious
form, that it is an orgiastic or ecstatic mode of primarily
unconscious experience. This disparaging attitude seems to
prevail even among the psychologically informed. It comes,
apparently, from the same human need that expresses itself
in feelings of excitement, awe, fear, fascination, or lust when
faced with the *mysterium*. It seems actually to arise from the
sense of the numinous (p. 126).

Laney was writing about Peyote, but why couldn't it apply to other
drugs as well? The feelings of excitement, awe, fear, and fascination
when faced with the mysterium, resembles a brief experience I once
had. At the time, the ignominious injections of methamphetamine was
my elixir, which have similar deleterious affects to the mind and body
as the chronic and addictive use of cocaine. After having been in a
sleepless imbroglio for three or four days and nights, my friend stopped
her car in front of my house. When I asked where she was going, she
told me that she was going to see her ex-boyfriend. She asked if I
wanted to go with her. As soon as she asked, I felt an overwhelming
sense of *excitement, awe, fear, and fascination*. This cerebral/emotional
paroxysm also had a physical quality—a throbbing, pins and needles
sensation throughout my body. The most numinous part of this maybe
fifteen second experience was fear. I could not say "No!" and get the
hell out of that car fast enough. Once I was inside of my house, I
remember saying to myself something like, "Wow! What was that all
about?" Pondering on the numinosity of that event since then, I have
passed if off as a diminished mental capacity—a drug induced quirk
coupled with sleep deprivation, *non compos mentis*—not of sound
mind. I still believe that to some degree, but I believe more that I had a
spiritual experience of some kind, perhaps an intuitive one. One that I
will probably never know the specific meaning or nature of. Sleep
deprivation, after several days and nights of injecting methamphetamine, has sent me on a number of cerebral excursions into the
numinosum—the negative numinosum, of course—a 'nonordinary
state of consciousness' is putting some of the experiences I had very
lightly.

Most addicts will assert that it was not their intention to grow up to be self-centered, hedonistic drug addicts and/or alcoholics. Nor was it their intention to personify the *puer* and/or trickster archetypes to accommodate that lifestyle. Nor was that my intention—(I don't think, at least not consciously). I'm not sure because when I was around six or seven years old, there was something about the *outlaw* that was compelling and attractive to me. However, during the same time period, when my playmates and I played cops and robbers, I always wanted to be the cop. At this early age I was already beginning to develop the structure of both poles of the *puer* and *senex* archetype. These consentaneous opposites are what is at the heart of addictive personalities. Hillman (1970) explains "that the senex is a complicatio of the *puer*, infolded into puer structure, so that *puer* events are complicated by a senex background" (p. 146). Most of my recent research prior to the trickster concerns the *puer* and *senex* archetypes, and it is my firm belief that in the chemically dependent population of our society, the structures of the *puer* and trickster begins to develop in childhood. I believe it did with me, anyway.

It might appear to some that I have shone a heterodox* light on the wide-spread view that the recreational use of chemical substances should be avoided. This is not my intention. Hopefully, my words won't be taken officiously. In most 12-step programs there is an expression that explains the general human condition when people voluntarily enter recovery programs, and that is incomprehensible demoralization. They are subjugated and they want to surrender. That was not the case with me. Unlike most 12-steppers, my life with drugs and alcohol was not incomprehensibly demoralizing. However, *quae nocent docent*, things that injure teach.

I believe I have been preordained to do something in my second life, but to accomplish it, I first had to attend the drug and alcohol school of the *puer* and trickster for over thirty years in my first life. Then, in order to earn the credibility to write and teach about what I learned in my first life, I had to go to more schools in my second life. Now that I am finished with the formal education of my second life, I am writing about the spiritual journey of my first life—and that, I think, is what I was preordained to do; hence, James Hillman's (1996) acorn theory, which proposes that "each life is formed by a particular image, an image that is the essence of that life and calls it to a destiny, just as the mighty oak's destiny is written in the tiny acorn." (inside flap)

---

* Heteron: *the other, otherness*. In Plato the Other is one of the major forms that pervades all the other forms, *Soph.* 255c-e. Some apparent nonbeing is merely the "other," *ibid.* 259a (see on). *Heteron* is a principle in the construction of World Soul (*Greek Philosophical Terms: A Historical Lexicon*).

Hopefully, my heterodox view of my first-life experiences will serve myself and others well— for at least as long as my second life lasts.

CHAPTER 8

ADDICTION, THE DISEASE CONCEPT, AND RECOVERY

W hat is Addiction? According to the DSM-IV, the essential feature of Substance Abuse "is a maladaptive pattern of substance use manifested by recurrent and significant adverse consequences related to the repeated use of substances." The essential feature of Substance Dependence, is a cluster of cognitive, behavioral, and physiological symptoms indicating that the individual continues the use of the substance despite significant substance-related problems. The DSM doesn't recognize the term 'addiction'. I do, and in my opinion the best definition of addiction is: ADDICTION IS A COMPULSION TO REPEAT A BEHAVIOR REGARDLESS OF ITS CONSEQUENCES. This definition is preferable because it covers a range of addictions beyond the scope of substances.

According to the Go Ask Alice website, a blanket statement concerning recovery from abuse and dependence reads as follows:

> Recovery rates from addiction follow a model of treatment outcomes applicable to most psychologically-based disorders: one-third recover fully; one-third cyclically stop their unhealthy behavior and return to it again; and one-third do not recover.*

Jointsters are addicts, and their addiction is more often a lifestyle than a physiological dependence. Statistics by the American Medical Association (AMA), and the DSM complicate matters here. We are talking about people who have dedicated their lives to the use of drugs and alcohol, and the recovery rates for them are very low—much lower

---

* See webpage (https://answers.google.com/answers/threadview?id=138544)

than what is stated above about abuse and dependence recovery rates.

I'm not saying that jointsters don't periodically get physically addicted to a substance. But what I am saying is that jointsters are more often *not* always physically addicted, depending on what drugs they are using of course. Heroin and cocaine are the most addictive psychologically and physically; however, whereas meth is highly addictive psychologically, it is not highly addictive physically. Marijuana isn't physically addictive either (except for maybe the new chemically treated marijuana), but it is certainly psychologically addictive. Therefore, it's more accurate to catagorize jointsters as *addicts*, based on their criminalized lifestyle and drug use, rather than categorizing all of them as being physically addicted.

Now, let's explore whether addiction is actually a disease or not.

THE DISEASE CONCEPT

Alcoholism was recognized as an illness by the American Medical Association in 1956. In 1966 they classified it as a *disease* because it meets the criteria of other diseases:

- It is chronic—it lasts a long time.
- It is progressive—it gets worse over time and can end with death.
- It is incurable—it can, however, be arrested by abstinence.
- It is primary—it is not just a symptom of some other underlying disorder.

In my opinion, the contention that addiction is a disease is simply conjecture. Just because the AMA says addiction is a disease, doesn't make it true.

- It is chronic—so is shoplifting, it lasts a long time.
- It is progressive—so is violence, it gets worse over time and can end with death.
- It is incurable—so is masturbating, however, it can be arrested by abstinence.
- It is primary—so is smoking cigarettes, it's not a symptom of another underlying disorder.

Still, the medical community and Americans in general have accepted the 'disease' concept and immediately used it for every aberrant behavior from alcohol consumption to masturbating. The disease concept was a remedy for faltering medical institutions, making available billions of dollars to the medical establishment and contributing to the growing evolution of pop-psychology.

The disease concept has infiltrated our society so thoroughly, perpetuating misinformation that damages the very people it was supposed to help. It is a disastrous situation where the theories of a few were assumed as fact by the medical community, without credible evidence. As a result, it wasn't long before the disease concept was accepted by the American public. Considering the history of the disease concept, we now have a better understanding of why it happened the way it did.

From physicians and their patients to drug manufacturers and the popular media, there is persistent pressure to categorize any condition as a disease. Physicians, particularly specialists, want to boost their credibility and standing in the medical community with 'groundbreaking declarations'—not to mention the income that arrives when a new condition is labeled as 'a disease'. Pharmaceutical companies have an obvious interest in making life's problems medical. Plus, alternative therapies such as holistic medicine and acupuncture are minimized, or dismissed as unscientific. Objectionable medical-ization is dangerous because of unnecessary labeling, inadequate treatment modalities, economic inefficiency, and the resulting costs when the available resources are diverted from treating or preventing more serious diseases. Addiction is the result of bad decisions, not a disease, and ignoring the bad decisions that addicts have made through the misuse of the disease concept, is perhaps part of the reason that treatment doesn't work.

DOES TREATMENT WORK?

Like those in 12-step programs, treatment professionals often claim success in the face of contradicting evidence. AA literature boasts; "Rarely have we seen a person fail who has thoroughly followed our path." The truth is, people rarely succeed when following the path of those in *all* 12-step programs. At least eighty percent of the existing treatment centers in the United States adhere to 12-Step philosophies. Not surprisingly, the success rate of treatment in rehabs is no different from the success rate of 12-step programs, counseling, psychotherapy, or analysis—which is approximately 3%.

While treatment professionals boast that *treatment works*, the question is, what is it exactly that's working? The assurance that treatment works does precious little for most people who drink or use too much. Of course, 12-step programs (treatment's alternative counterpart and co-conspirator), lead with the same misleading and outright assurance that their programs work. Twelve steppers conveniently claim success without any foundation. In reality the statement is a complete contradiction to empirical evidence. Both 12-step programs and treatment of *any* kind are outright failures when held to any standard but their own. But apparently it's a matter of semantics. It comes down to who is using the word *works*.

The public believing that these programs are *working* would be a testament to helping people with substance abuse issues get clean and sober. Said another way, those who join the groups can overcome their addiction. But, after arriving in treatment or a 12-step program with the hopes of overcoming their addiction, those in need are told that they can never get well because there is no cure. So, what is it exactly that's working?

With that said, the various recovery options available are all we have; therefore, it would be indiscreet to say that they are a waste of time. Until someone discovers the magic bullet, we're left with what is available. I have attended 12-step meetings since 1990 and am still clean and sober today. I don't read the literature, I don't have a higher power, I don't share in meetings, and I don't use a sponsor. However, my journey of recovery has been made easier by attending meetings where I have been able to listen to people who are like me. What I don't agree with, I leave there, and take the rest with me.

A commonly heard cliche around twelve-step programs is "We are not bad people trying to get good, we are sick people trying to get better." Having previously surveyed an archetypal *understanding of the lived experiences* of criminalized drug addicts, this chapter will now go so far as to propose that they are neither bad or sick people. They're just people who have made bad decisions that predisposed them to personify the *puer* and/or trickster archetypes in order to accommodate a lifestyle created by those bad decisions. This personification is caused in myriad ways when we are indoctrinated into the mind-set associated with substance use.

It is often argued however, that the combination of adolescent peer pressure and substance use lies in what Christina Grof calls *A Thirst for Wholeness*. My suggestion in Chapter Two that peers are a source of *adolescent self-actualization* is similar to Frankel's suggestion that getting high offers them an *experiential transcendence*.

So, are all of these people really sick? If they are, maybe we should start an "anonymous" program for those who are not sick (normies anonymous), because they seem to be in the minority. Apparently, there is something to be said about Weil's contention that the desire to alter consciousness periodically is an innate, normal drive, because all those *anonymous* behaviors alter consciousness to some degree. Who wouldn't, for example, like to walk around with a perpetual orgasm—as long as we could function normally at the same time. That would be the epitome of altering consciousness. Everybody would like that, but not everybody would like to be addicted to all the addictive behaviors covered in the gamut of 12-step programs and in the offices of psychologists. Therefore, we are dealing not with something socially or culturally based but rather with a part-biological, part-archetypal characteristic of the species.

Besides, the need for altering consciousness begins at ages far too young for it to be caused by social conditioning alone. Kids playing, alter consciousness frequently, such as three to five year-olds spinning themselves into dizziness. I remember when I was ten or eleven years old, my friends and I would squeeze each other around the chest after inhaling and exhaling several times. Then we would lose consciousness and flop around on the floor like a fish out of water. I believe that this deep need to alter consciousness reflects our natural desire to transcend our quotidian ego-centered identity and experience something more. When these changes of consciousness interfere with normal functioning, then we need to find direction.

Many people refuse treatment for alcoholism or drug addiction because they don't believe they are sick. I agree. They are not bad and they are not sick. They need to either personify different archetypes or redirect the energies of the old ones, and they need to alter consciousness in different ways. I assert that what is needed is a path to recovery from, not the *disease* of addiction, but just from addiction. Cigarette smoking is also an addiction, but it isn't labeled a disease. Drugs and alcohol however, are deterrents to wholeness that stifle our individuation.

Millions of people have recovered with the help of 12-step programs. There are also millions of people who have recovered by other means such as psychotherapy and/or religion. Many have even stopped using substances on their own through what is known in medical circles as spontaneous remission. However, there are others who could and would glean the many benefits of 12-step programs if they weren't bombarded with religious concepts, and having the disease concept shoved down their throats.

I am proposing a model for recovery employing the ancient art/science of alchemy—a model I have developed which includes elements borrowed from 12 step programs. I also explain a method that

I *thought* I invented when I was in prison, but later discovered was a process already practiced in cognitive psychology. This technique is called 'thought-stopping', which, amongst other things, is what worked for me.

WHAT IS ALCHEMY?

Many of us are drawn to the mysteries of the past to enlighten the quality of the present. Mythology, astrology, the tarot, runes, and I-Ching have drawn the interest of many in recent years, and are being enjoyed and utilized in fresh and innovative ways. Ancient wisdom imbued by myths, legends and symbols can generate transformation, and transformation is what alchemy is all about. More commonly known as the art of transforming base metal into gold, few people realize what a vast philosophical foundation this early science has. Alchemy is a process that continues to grow and expand, offering deeper understanding and awareness, and has a profound potential to change lives. This fountain of ancient wisdom has nourished seekers of spiritual enlightenment throughout the ages.

The first material of alchemy, the prima materia (primal material), is a base substance known by many but recognized only by the esoteric. The outward form of the prima materia must be destroyed because it is pure chaos. Treatment of the prima materia in the alchemical vessel by heat leads to its death, a moment known as the 'nigredo,' or blackening. With a methodical treatment and heat, the prima materia 'whitens,' indicating that the elixir is perfected in its first degree, a moment known as the 'albedo,' or whitening. To attain the gold-promising tincture of the sun, further treatment is necessary until the elixir reddens, which is referred to as the 'rubedo.' There is also a 'citrinitas,' which is a yellowing in the ancient process, but this isn't used in most texts that delineate the alchemical process, especially the psychological and philosophical treatises.

Correlating this to the process of recovery from addiction, the alchemical process transforms consciousness, which is the endeavor of depth psychology. When non-Jungians study Carl Jung's concept of the transference, they are often struck by how heavily it draws on alchemical symbolism. I won't be focusing much on alchemical symbolism in my approach, but transference is always an issue between sponsors and the people they sponsor in 12-step programs.

In a way, sponsorship is practicing psychotherapy without a license or the supporting education. Unlike therapists however, sponsors aren't paid for it. Members of 12-step programs have been practicing psychotherapy without a license since the 30s under the guise of sponsorship. With this model of psychotherapeutic transformation through the alchemical process, recovery can be achieved using my modified version of the steps, which I call 'stages of development'. I have also substituted the word *advocate* for sponsor and the word *partisan* for sponsee. Note that I am not claiming by any means, that *The Alchemical Approach to Recovery* is any better than any other approach or model, and I am certainly not claiming that it will be any more successful. This is not the magic bullet. It's just an option for those who have issues with traditional 12-step programs such as the program's emphasis on God and/or higher power, the disease concept, sharing in meetings, or the tenets of 12-step literature.

History

Alchemy has a history stretching back at least 2,500 years and has been practiced in Eastern, Arabic and Western societies. Historically, alchemists were more interested in the chemical techniques, others in the philosophical aspects, and some saw alchemy as a path to the true meaning of Christianity, while others saw the possibilities of producing medicines and other concoctions. For a more in depth coverage of alchemy, I recommend Jeffrey Raff's *Jung and the Alchemical Imagination* and Marie-Louise von Franz's *Alchemy*.

Twelve-step programs however, have a much shorter history, originating in 1935 when two alcoholics, Dr. Bob Smith and Bill Wilson met. From two people to millions just in AA, not to mention all the other 12-step programs, the 12-steps are now universally known. Carl Jung had a key role in the founding of AA, and he has written extensively on the psychologically and spiritually transformational aspects of alchemy.

As I stated previously, the following formula for recovery is for those who take issue with 12-step programs, or for those who would simply like to try another model. However, I am not suggesting that meetings be eliminated. Recovering alcoholics and addicts need to be continually reminded of what got them into the recovery process in the first place. Besides that, most of us are more comfortable around people with backgrounds similar to ours. We identify with other addicts. The best advice I've heard concerning meetings is "take what you can identify with and leave the rest there." Too many people stop attending meetings because they don't like what they're hearing or who they're hearing it from. It's best to make every attempt to listen to the message rather than the messenger, and seek the similarities rather than the differences of those who share in meetings. If 12-step meetings aren't an option, there are other types of support groups available such as Rational Recovery.

THE ALCHEMICAL PROCESS OF RECOVERY

The mercurial spirit of the prima materia is otherwise known as chaos, and those entering the recovery process certainly fit that description. It is the job of the alchemist to kill the prima materia and in the process the prima materia turns into the blackening state of nigredo. This sets the stage for a transformation—the first conuinctio (conjunction).

The first conuinctio begins when the ego (consciousness) discovers the reality of the unconscious psyche and makes an effort to pay attention to it. If recovery is being sought for intrinsic purposes, then the ego has acknowledged an unconscious need; therefore, the first conuinctio is the transformation from the dregs of active addiction to the *clamor* of abstinence (and I emphasize clamor because early abstinence is often as chaotic as active addiction). This part of the transformation is tentative and unstable, and the most susceptible for relapse.

The second conuinctio is the transformation from abstinence to recovering. What was previously only an ideal becomes a living reality. This stage of recovering can be thought of as the whitening of the albedo—the ego having reached a new level of being. At this new level of consciousness, the addict (which includes the alcoholic), now has hope.

The third conuinctio is the transformation from recovering to recovered. This can take many years, and sometimes it never happens. This is when the contents of the alchemical vessel has turned to gold. This is when individuation of the alchemical process has been achieved, also referred to as the philosopher's stone. Of course, there are those who stay in the abstinence stage (albedo) indefinitely, and a regression can happen during any stage of the transformation. There are also those who return to the chaos of the prima materia that existed prior to their entry into the recovery process, which is translated as a relapse back into chaos.

APPLICATION

The main purpose of advocacy is to guide the prospective partisan through the process. There are many approaches to this. When a prospect asks someone to be their advocate, the advocate sets the parameters of the advocacy. Here's a crude example I might consider using with a prospect with an arrogant and inflated ego: Ask the prospect to squat down and quack like a duck around a baseball diamond. If he tells me where to stick the baseball diamond, then I won't be his advocate. Outlaw motorcycle gangs and college fraternities do similar things for similar reasons. Here's a more practical one: I might ask the prospect to spend an entire day with me with an egg in his pocket (not a hard-boiled one either) without breaking it. The purpose is to demonstrate how fragile our recovery is. Advocates can use their imagination with this. There is no point in an advocate investing so much time and effort in someone unless that someone is willing to go to any lengths to recover. Anyway, once the prospect has been accepted for advocacy, the first homework assignment will be for him or her to read *The Elements of Alchemy* by Cherry Gilchrist.

THE TEN STAGES OF DEVELOPMENT

The first conuinctio has gotten the prospect to abstinence and to counseling, or some kind of support group and/or recovery process. If recovery is being sought for intrinsic purposes, then the ego has acknowledged an unconscious need. Before the transformation to the second conuinctio can occur, he or she needs to get an advocate and start going through the process of recovery. There is no specific schedule or time limit for this process, but the stages should develop in sequence.

Many of those seeking recovery with an advocate using the alchemical method, are the ones who have issues with the traditional Christian sky-God—that is, the agnostics and atheists. The 12-steps are fraught with the word God, so the word God doesn't appear in the 10 stages of development. I have made other changes in wording and process to conform to the alchemical approach. Anyone who tries this approach is encouraged to make any adaptive changes that might suit those who are participating, for this is a theoretical model with room for improvement—a work in progress.

Stage One: Admit that I have a problem.

This is essential, and needs to happen first. While still in the nigredo state, the prospect must admit he has a problem. He will actually be working on this when an alchemical oriented advocate interviews him as a prospect, and this is when the advocate makes an attempt to determine whether the prospect's reasons for being in recovery are intrinsic or extrinsic. If he is in the process as a result of a nudge from the judge, to get his wife back, to save his job, or for any other extrinsic purpose, then they shouldn't go any farther until the advocate is thoroughly convinced that the prospect is there for himself. When the advocate is finally convinced, then the prospect becomes a partisan.

The advocate, after discussing other criteria for advocacy, will then give the following homework assignment.

* Have you seriously damaged or destroyed relationships with friends because of your addiction? If you have, write down those relationships and how you damaged them.

* If you've been told by others how you hurt them, put it on paper.

* Write down how and when you have damaged or destroyed relationships with your loved ones in order to indulge in your addiction.

* Write down any illnesses that your addiction has caused.

* Write down occasions when you expressed anger toward others.

* Write down incidents in your life related to your addiction that caused you to be embarrassed or humiliated.

* Put in writing any times in the past that you tried to control your addiction, and mention how successful or unsuccessful each time was.

* Are you sorry for the ways that you have acted during your addiction? If you are, put it on paper.

* Write down any irrational or crazy set of events that have happened since you began your addiction. If you rationalized this behavior, write down how.

* Put in writing how you have avoided others because they disapproved of your addiction. Also include who they were and the circumstances.

* Pinpoint on paper exactly when your life started to deteriorate, and what was going on in your life at that time.

* Write down exactly what made you realize that you had a problem, and why you couldn't control it.

* Read *Scumbag Sewer Rats* by John Smethers, Ph.D.

The partisan really needs to know how much work this process is going to be and how long it's going to take. If he or she reads this book and still wants to continue, then the advocacy can continue.

Stage Two: Presume that my problem will be resolved.

An image of higher power is not required but I suggest recognizing some type of universal force, even if it can't be identified. The partisan can use anything he or she wants, or can use a support group-of-choice, since this approach will likely be used primarily by non-religious addicts. Once the partisan really believes a group, a force, and/or his advocate, can resolve his problem, they will then begin to see the blackening contents of the alchemical vessel starting to whiten. The advocate will then assign the following as homework.

* Put on paper what religion you grew up with, and the pros and cons of that religion.

* Write down any dreams that you have had about forces or gods, and describe what they meant to you.

* Mythology isn't just a collection of random stories about gods and goddesses. There are parallels to real life scenarios in all myths if you look for them. Read *Parallel Myths* by J. F. Bierlein.

Stage Three: Make a moral inventory.

Stages three and four involves major action. Stage three is an inventory which prepares the partisan for the next stage. This inventory should include not only the deep dark immoral secrets of hedonistic and scandalous turpitude, but also the more admirable traits that have often gone unnoticed. Homework assignment:

* Write down what broken relationships with the opposite sex or friends you have had, and explain how those broken relationships hurt them and/or you. Note any anger or resentments concerning these relationships.

* Write down when you have acted self-righteously, and whether you believed you were justified and why.

* Put in writing what influenced you to start drinking or using.

* Write down specific situations, emotions, experiences, and the people you associated with before your addictive mind-set and lifestyle began.

* Write down all the grudges you held and if you got revenge, and include whether or not anyone was hurt.

* Put on paper what you hate most in others, and whether you have any of these traits?

* Put on paper any dreams you've had concerning the work you've done during this stage.

Stage Four: Disclose to my advocate all misconduct during my addiction.

All of those despicable things that the partisan has done during his or her addiction have been kept a secret, and needs to be examined. If he or she doesn't wish to disclose those things with their advocate, then the advocacy is stalled. Most advocates, however, during their addiction, have done most of the things that their partisans have done, if not worse, so there's really not a valid reason to refuse to disclose misconduct of the past, especially after the advocate discloses some of his or her past. Homework assignment:

   *   After having completed all third stage homework, write down what you have come to realize concerning your limitations and capabilities.

   *   Put in writing what the disclosure of the fourth stage was like, and what your feelings were before, during, and after the process. List what the reasons are for doing this?

   *   Write down why myth is a constant among all human beings in all times (answer is in the *Parallel Myths*).

   Usually by this time, the advocate will have already witnessed the contents of the alchemical vessel transform from the blackening of the nigredo to the whitening of the albedo. The advocate will discuss with him at what point of the alchemical process he believes he is at. If he has internalized his recovery thus far as an alchemical process and recognizes the importance of the transformation of the second conuinctio, then they can continue their journey of transformation. Hopefully the partisan has internalized the death of his old self and the birth of the new. The benefit of the third and fourth stages, if the partisan has been successful, is the completion of the second conuinctio—the whitening of the alchemical vessel has turned red. He is in the rubedo phase, and some kind of Rite of Passage is pertinent.

   12-step programs recognize various lengths of recovery. In the alchemical process of recovery, receiving chips is eliminated until after the fourth stage is complete, which is when a Rite of Passage for the 2nd conuinctio occurs. If the advocate doesn't believe that his partisan has actually achieved the 2nd conuinctio, then he should consider discontinuing advocacy or re-evaluating it considerably. However, if the 2nd conuinctio has been achieved, then the partisan can start getting annual chips if he or she wants to.

   To ignore rites of passage or dismiss them as trivial or unnecessary rituals, is as ridiculous as accepting 'denial' as being a river in Africa. It is stated on The Stanton Peele Addiction website that;

   Of the Jewish people the sociologists actually interviewed, none had ever had a drinking problem. Investigating all reports by activists in the Jewish community who had announced a growing alcoholism problem, Glassner and Berg could not actually locate one Jewish alcoholic. Accepting at

face values all such reports led to calculation of an alcoholism
rate of about one-tenth of one percent among Jewish adults.

Could it be that a bar mitzvah is responsible for this? Perhaps—at
least where drugs and alcohol are concerned. However, judging by
reports from the Jewish community, they do have other addictions such
as overeating and anorexia. According to the National Jewish Press,
Ross (April, 1986) reports that there are "seven to 10 thousand Jewish
inmates in the United States." Though that number has undoubtedly
increased since then, it would probably still be a very small percentage
of the more than two million Americans that are behind bars today.
Under the aegis of the church, could initiatory rites of passage account
for the absence of addiction in Jewish culture? If so, what about other
cultures?

"The term initiation," as defined by Eliade (1958) "in the most
general sense denotes a body of rites and oral teachings whose purpose
is to produce a decisive alteration in the religious and social status of
the person to be initiated" (p. x). The closest I came to being elevated
from a child to something more than a child, was when I left grammar
school and entered junior high. With only a short graduation ceremony
from the elementary school level, what followed came as a radical
social change. In what seems now like an almost overnight transformation, I went from a pleasant grade school boy to an acerbic junior high
school rebel without a cause: from playing on the monkey bars to
getting drunk at Friday night football games; from wrestling with
schoolmates on the playground to gang fights with rival Mexican
gangs—riotous, no doubt, just like the Germanic berserkers of
antiquity; from playing hide-and-go-seek with girls to whisking them
out of the movie theater to kiss and fondle them—not unlike the
mythological Theseus carrying off Adriadne; from recess to smoking in
the bath rooms during breaks; from evenings home with parents to
malicious mischief in the neighborhood with friends. It could be argued
that there is a nexus between our malicious mischief, addiction, and the
spirit of initiation. My friends and I felt compelled to prove ourselves
to each other, so we acted-out an incredible amount of destructive
behavior in the process. This seemingly overnight transformation from
boy to renegade, wasn't observed as such by my parents because the
changes to them were slow and subtle.

My elementary school graduation happened at about the same age
as the bar mitzvah does in Jewish culture, which is the time of life when
change naturally occurs, so it is the ideal time for a rite of passage.

Being unfamiliar with the bar mitzvah and what their ordeals entail, I believe it is safe to assume that painstaking lengths are taken to ensure some kind of enduring conversion. Eliade (1958) says that among the Australian Yuin tribe "the first initiation ceremony, comprising the separation from the women and the ordeal by fire, is thus complete. From that night on the novices share only in the life of the *men*" (p.8). Indeed, the elevation to junior high school with its incumbent social status seemed to suddenly sever an emotional attachment to my parents, and created a different kind of emotional attachment to my newly acquired friends—friends, I might add, some of whom I kept for more than 30 years and still have today. Obviously, that pubescent ceremony was not in any way doing what a rite of passage should do. In discussing "the secret society of the Bakhimba in Mayombe," Eliade shares that "the initiatory ordeals continue from two to five years" (p. 75).

Considering the Jewish rites of passage, and similar rites in other cultures, I believe my point is well taken that a significant rite of passage is a life-changing event; however, although the most opportune time is at the pubescent stage, it can still occur anytime during human development. The *puer* archetype has enabled the addict to remain in adolescent psychology. A rite of passage needs to occur to elevate the *puer* or *puella* to maturity. A chip and a cake is not enough—especially the redundancy of repeating it every year. It will be between the advocate and the partisan to come up with a rite of passage significant enough to cement an enduring transformation in the life of the partisan, and I suggest incorporating something monumental. Possibly something like the Bakhimba in Mayombe, which lasts from two to five years. Or, perhaps something that doesn't take as long, but requires more effort, such as a vision quest in the mountains alone for a week.

Stage Five: Work on eliminating my character flaws.

The rubedo is the third stage and its color is red. Red was thought by alchemists to contain the essence of life. Medieval people believed that the soul resided in the blood, and the heart was therefore the spiritual and physical center of a person's life. From here on, the emphasis on change increases considerably. The partisan has only one *thing* to change, and that's every*thing*, so all the baggage he or she is carrying around from the past needs to be disposed of. Homework:

    *   Are there any fairy tales or myths that you found in *Parallel Myths* that you have a special affinity for? Write down which ones and why.

* Put in writing situations and events where your pride was glaring, and what this brought into your life that you like and dislike. Also write down the problems it has caused you.

* Write down activities you especially enjoy (excepting drug and alcohol consumption).

* Write down a few healthy eating or exercise habits that you could start, and some unhealthy eating habits that you could give up.

* Note some secret 'good' deeds that you have done or that you would like to do.

* Put on paper occasions where you have been greedy, excessively needy, or materialistic.

* Write down situations where you have given in to lust without regard for others, and note the problems that it caused you.

* Write down when or wherever your inner trickster has been dishonest, the problems it caused you, and whether you are ready to allow your advocate or group or a force to help keep you honest and direct your trickster proclivities in a more productive direction.

* Put in writing situations when you have been envious or jealous of others, what problems it has caused you, and whether you are ready to discuss these situations with others.

* Write down situations where you have avoided being responsible for your actions or lack of actions, and the problems it has caused you. Include whether you are ready to allow your advocate and/or a group or some type of force to help you take responsibility for your actions?

* Put on paper your major character flaws, and what you plan to do when these flaws begin to manifest. Note each flaw individually along with the proposed preventive behavior and how you will allow a group and/or your advocate to help in your battle against these flaws.

* Write down any dreams you've had that you could relate to your character flaws.

* Discuss on paper any myths that compare to your character flaws.

Timing is an essential factor in inner alchemy. Twelve-steppers have noticed repeatedly that a member will hear something clearly only when the time is right, which is another reason why partisans should attend some type of support group. Advocates may continually point out something with no results. Then later, the partisan informs him that he or she has discovered a great truth that is exactly what the advocate had been trying to get across all along. Timing is a great mystery, for it cannot be controlled by us. At a certain moment, an experience that would have been impossible a week before unfolds with no difficulty. The alchemists warned that all haste was of the devil; being in a hurry violates the gradual evolution that accords with time. As the Chinese philosophers well knew, to be in accord with the time makes the difference between success and failure. It's not conducive to our recovery to beat ourselves up when his happens, but it is conducive to our recovery to listen to what's being said in groups, by advocates, teachers and spiritual gurus, which is why it is more important to listen to the message rather than the messenger when attending meetings of any kind.

*   Put on paper what you have heard in meetings or groups that you have actually chosen to ignore because you didn't like who was speaking.
*   Write down the character flaws that will be most difficult to give up, and place them in what order you plan to give them up.
*   Put in writing the types of situations, stressors or pressures that cause you to regress back into your character flaws, and what you can do to lessen the likelihood of that stress occurring.
*   Write down what makes you lose hope and whether you can avoid those situations, and include what person(s), situation(s), event(s), or thought(s) restores your hope.
*   Be specific when you write about how you think your life will be different without your character flaws.
*   Write down what you are grateful for (I've heard it said that grateful people are happy people ☺).
*   Jot down when you were the happiest and why.
*   Put in writing your typical day's activities in terms of how much time you spend on each type of activity. Write down what you would do in a typical day if you knew that you had only one year to live.
*   Write down how much time you would like to spend with loved ones.
*   Put on paper what you can do to contribute to the *anima mundi* (soul of the world)—making it a better place to live.

Stage Six: Document all the people I have mistreated.

Stages six and seven are imperative for an enduring peace of mind, and essential for the third conuinctio. It's very unlikely that anyone can live a happy and productive life if they're living with how they've mistreated others. The third conuinctio is our final destination, but we have the rest of our lives to sustain it. The third conuinctio is the philosopher's stone, individuation of the recovery process, the hypothetical Gold at the end of the rainbow. Like the Bakhimba in Mayombe, the third conuinctio should take from two to five years, with a rite of passage more imposing than that of the second conuinctio. Homework:

* Put in writing all the people that you have mistreated by your addiction, and the effect on them and on you and on your relationship with them.

* Write down what you could do to make up for what you've done to each of them, and the consequences you fear in accomplishing this. Include the worst and the best things that can happen, and what you think will happen.

* Write down whether you feel angry or resentful toward any people that you have mistreated? If so, write them a letter of anger, but don't send it.

* Put in writing any other ways that you have used to get rid of anger and resentment toward those you have mistreated.

* Write down any dreams that relate to how you've mistreated others.

Stage Seven: Make up for how I mistreated others whenever the opportunity arises.

Of course, don't try reconciliation if it will cause injury to them or anyone else. Once every person who has been mistreated is documented, along with the essential homework in connection with it, then the partisan is ready to start a process that sometimes takes years. This is one of those stages that doesn't always get finished, but it's necessary to stay conscious of it and apply it whenever the opportunity arises. Homework:

* Put on paper what you have done so far to make up for how you've mistreated others? These can include apologies, helpful tasks for those that you have mistreated, changed attitudes, etc. Remember, this work is *more* than just apologies, but sometimes an apology is all you can do.

* Write down if there are apologies that you need to make that doesn't require reconciliation and why.

* Rehearse reconciliations by using the *imaginal dialogues* discussed in Chapter One.

* Read to a friend and your advocate what you've done so far toward reconciliation, and ask if it sounds sincere enough. Write down what responses they have about them.

* After you have had your first encounter, write down what

happened, how you felt about it, how the other person responded, what you learned from it, and what you would do differently next time.

* After having made up for mistreating others, write down your overall impressions, whether anything surprised or disappointed you, and which ones will be the most difficult to accomplish.

* Write down how you are dealing with having to defend yourself?

* Have you had any dreams about reconciliation to those you've mistreated? If so, describe them in detail on paper.

* Describe in writing the conversation(s) in your imaginal dialogues.

* Find at least one myth containing a comparison to reconciliation.

Yes, intrinsic, lasting recovery is a lot of work.

Stage Eight: Learn to admit when I'm wrong.

Most of us have a natural tendency to *not* admit when we're wrong. The philosopher's stone cannot be achieved unless we are able to do this—despite how embarrassing or humiliating it might be, or how much it deflates our egos.

Individuation of the recovery process is a status that not all, even many recovered people, actually achieve. How can an advocate elevate his partisan to the ultimate level if the partisan is still operating on an external locus of control. The philosopher's stone—the Gold—cannot be achieved unless an internal locus of control has been accomplished. If we place blame 'out there' and not take ownership of our part in it, then we are in an *ex*ternal locus of control. If we are truly accountable for all of our actions and are unhesitatingly willing to admit when we're wrong, then we can say that we are operating on an internal locus of control. But this is a process. We get better and better at it as time progresses, providing we are actively and continually working on it. Homework:

* Put in writing a plan to allow time for reflection each day, and write down some of your imaginal dialogues and who they were with?

* Write down new behaviors you would like to try to make your alchemical journey of recovery more effective, and how you will go about implementing these.

* Discuss on paper the 'stinking thinking' that so many recovering addicts have such a hard time letting go of, and include what strategies you plan to use to avoid it.

* Write down all of your triggers for addictive behavior, and how you can guard against them or prepare for them.

* Put in writing any dreams in connection with this stage of development.

Stage Nine: Improve my relationship with humanity through introspection and imaginal dialogues.

If we were contumacious assholes during our addiction, then this stage serves as a monitor to keep us in check so we won't be that way anymore. Everybody needs introspection, but far from everybody participates in this spiritual notion. The world we live in can be viewed as hostile or amicable. We cannot achieve individuation of the recovery process we desire—the philosopher's stone—if we don't view our fellow men and women as partners rather than antagonists. Life isn't a contest. Homework:

   * If you nip something in the bud, you deal with a problem when it is still small, before it can grow into something serious. Put in writing a time when your life started heading in the wrong direction and you were able to nip it in the bud.

   * Put on paper how you would describe your overall outlook and beliefs concerning humanity.

   * Write down your favorite sources of wisdom and knowledge about healthy values.

   * If you were stranded on a desert island with only one book, jot down which one it would be and why.

   * Put in writing your imaginal dialogues during this stage of your development.

   * If you had only one week to live with unlimited resources, write down who you would prefer to be with, and how you would pass the time.

   * Write a detailed account of what you would like your obituary to say.

Stage Ten: Having experienced a spiritual awakening, I will help other addicts, and practice what I've learned.

After having attended AA and NA for several years, I only had a vague understanding of what a spiritual awakening or spiritual experience was. As a research project when I was working on my doctorate, I interviewed and tape-recorded addicts and alcoholics, asking them to explain their spiritual experiences. The following chapter is that research project. Homework for stage ten:

   * Put in writing how you have been able to reach out to another recovering addict, then describe the situation and how it felt to you.

   * Discuss on paper how you usually handle various types of conflict, and any ways that you can think of to be more effective in

conflict resolution.

   *   Do you want to become an advocate? Write down the reasons why or why not.

   *   Write down how much time you are willing to devote to working with others in their recovery.

   *   Put in writing what inner or outer resources you can call on when you need help as an advocate (imaginal dialogues and active imagination are inner practical resources).

   *   Explain on paper any dreams you've had where you were in service to others.

Once the ten stages of development and the third conuinctio is complete, which can take several years, the addict has achieved individuation of the recovery process. The contents of the alchemical vessel has turned into Gold. He or she has become the philosopher's stone. In 12-step jargon, he or she has recovered from a seemingly hopeless case of mind and body. Again, the alchemical imagery and processes will continue to be used, and hopefully the partisan will also have found a life worth living and an enduring interest in the spiritual aspects of recovery, of alchemical transformation, and in alchemy in general. This is the time when the final rite of passage has been completed—a monumental undertaking—one that can nourish serenity for the rest of the partisan's life. Examples of this final rite of passage are the vision quest (like that suggested for the second conuinctio), where the partisan spends a week alone in the mountains or desert away from civilization; a day of fasting every week for a year; writing a book; or taking a year or so to further develop the alchemical approach to recovery. Whatever it is, it must be something that elevates the partisan to an ontological and epistemological level that he or she is not willing to give up *no matter what*!

THOUGHT STOPPING

This process comes from my personal experience. I will start by discussing dope-fiend mentality at the time I was sentenced to state prison. It was my intention to do my time, get out and serve a 13-month parole, then return to what I knew best and what I was the most comfortable with—doing drugs and alcohol as a way of life. Upon release from prison, the average parole is from three to four years, depending on performance while on parole. However there are exceptions. Sometimes a parolee can get off in 13 months, provided he does not have any brushes with the law and has not given his parole officer a single dirty urinalysis. I had two friends who achieved this.

A few months after I reached the prison yard where I was to remain for the rest of my sentence, it occurred to me that I could probably use lessons on how to stay clean—even if it was only going to be for 13 months. I started attending NA meetings. After attending for a while, a residential substance-abuse education program for pre-release inmates in their last 60 days started, it was called Project Change. To fill bed-space when it began, they had to accept people with more than 60 days left on their sentence. I interviewed for a place in the program and was accepted—still having six months left of my sentence.

About a month later, because of my typing skills, I landed a job with the program as a clerk. I typed questionnaires, tests and quizzes, inventory sheets—all kinds of material gleaned from recovery books. After working as a clerk for awhile, something started to happen: I started taking the program more seriously. I actually started thinking about possibly remaining permanently clean after my release.

Recovery for me started when I was a clerk in Project Change. Most of us jointsters are human garbage cans when it comes to drugs and alcohol. Achieving recovery without any help from recovery programs or self-help groups or counseling is often a pyrrhic victory over addiction; referred to below as 'a process of natural recovery' and known as 'spontaneous remission' in the medical profession.

In the CORK Bibliography on the Internet, Granfield states that "two dimensions of natural recovery that have important implications for treatment providers are: (1) the common strategies used by the subjects, (2) the concept of 'recovery capital' in terms of personal attributes and social environments that contribute to recovery."

Spontaneous remission from drug addiction is something that is not acknowledged much in the literature. Though I had Project Change and NA to bolster my emerging recovery, those who would rather strike out on their own to recover could try some of the jointster creativity that I employed in the joint. This process could be thought of as a spontaneous remission if there were no outside forces influencing those who use it. Or, it can be used concomitantly with other methods of recovery .

It occurred to me while I was in prison that if I was going to remain clean and sober when I hit the streets, I was going to have to change my thinking. I spent every waking hour either thinking about the bar I used to work in, the people I drank and used with, and the women I slept with. I remembered a video that stated "if lasting change is going to take place, one has to monitor and discipline one's thought processes."

That made a lot of sense to me, so I decided to shoo those old

thoughts away—literally, and replace them with different thoughts—
more productive thoughts. I say literally, because with my hand moving
in a swooshing motion by my ear, I shooed the thoughts away. Walking
around the big yard shooing thoughts away in that manner, I could tell
by the looks I was getting that I was being viewed through jaundiced
eyes. "Look at that freak," they must have thought. I didn't care what
they thought. I was never going to ever see any of them again anyway—
once I was released.

At first it took me a long time to remember to shoo those ever-
present thoughts away, so I only did it two or three times a day at
first—whenever I could remember. As time passed, I started
remembering more often and doing it more, and more, until I was doing
it a lot. That's when I started getting so many of *the looks* from fellow
prisoners. After awhile I discovered that I wasn't doing it as often. Day
by day I did it less and less. And then, guess what? After about four or
five months I completely exorcized those thoughts from my mind and
replaced them with thoughts of what I wanted to be doing when I got
out.

I visualized myself in NA meetings, and I visualized myself in
college classrooms. I also visualized taking care of my aged and ailing
mother. Upon my release, I did all of those things. And thanks to Kathy,
a teacher in the Project Change program who took a special interest in
my academic ability, nagged me until I agreed to enroll in college, then
she helped me fill out all of those tedious financial aid forms.

To be sure, my modified version of the steps through the alchemical
process is only a model for those who take issue with 12-step programs.
Meetings are just one element of a 12-step program, they are not *the*
program. One doesn't need to be a member to benefit from meetings.
Take me for example. Since my release from prison in December 1989
I have attended meetings, but I don't share in meetings, I don't use a
sponsor, I don't have a higher power, I don't believe in the disease
concept, and I don't agree with much of the literature. I do believe
however, that meetings contributed significantly to my recovery
because of the education I received by listening to others share, and by
making new friends.

ARCHETYPES & CULTURE

The wounded healer is an archetypal dynamic that may be constellated
in a helping relationship. Whereas sponsors in 12-step programs or
advocates in the alchemical approach aren't licensed like psychothera-
pists and counselors, what we often have in common is a relationship

with those we advocate for. This lasts for years, and sometimes the duration of our lives. The term *wounded healer* derives from the mythological Asclepius, a Greek doctor who in recognition of his own wounds established a sanctuary at Epidaurus where others could be healed of their wounds. The wounded healers in the alchemical process of recovery are advocates, and advocates are addicts, and addicts personify predominately two archetypes—the *puer aeternus* and the trickster; therefore, advocates should educate their partisans of those archetypes during the advocacy.

By integrating the alchemical process of recovery with the thought-stopping process, along with a combined knowledge of the archetypes, and whatever additional tools that become available to a recovering addict, he or she will likely have had, or will have had, some kind of spiritual awakening or experience that Carl Jung said was so vitally necessary for recovery.

CHAPTER 9

VARIETIES
OF SPIRITUAL EXPERIENCE

Twelve step meetings were where I gathered this variety of spiritual experiences. I collected these experiences over the course of a summer. I found that a range of these experiences came from a simple realization that change had to take place in order for recovery to ensue; to bright lights and ecstatic feelings; to revelations with God.

When the 12-step leader asked for a topic in meetings, (and in order to learn what I wanted to know), I asked those who had had spiritual experiences to please share about them. I also approached members after meetings and during breaks. The ones who were friends, I went to their homes. Though most of my research was collected in Barstow, I also ventured to other communities in the high desert.

The Big Book of *Alcoholic's Anonymous* (1976) states, "we have had deep and effective spiritual experiences that have revolutionized our whole attitude toward life, toward our fellows and toward God's universe" (p. 25). Later it states, "if when drinking, you have little control over the amount you take, you are probably alcoholic. If that be the case, you may be suffering from an illness which only a spiritual experience will conquer" (p. 44).

For most of my life, I have been somewhat of an iconoclast, since I don't recognize a traditional God figure or higher power. During my attendance in 12-step meetings over the first several years of my recovery, I only had a vague understanding of what was meant in the previous quotes about spiritual experience, or what people in meetings meant by it. I was aware of various perceptions of God, for 12-steppers believe that they can develop a God of their own understanding, and I was also aware of religious experiences such as the burning bush described in the Book of Exodus. I limited my interactions with recovered alcoholics and drug addicts to one request: that they explain a spiritual awakening or experience that was conducive to their recovery.

Rather than going into a discourse in hermeneutics, I will offer some definitions. The *Webster's* definition for spiritual is: "1. of the spirit or the soul. 2. of sacred matters; religious." We have a slight ambiguity here differentiating between religious and secular. In Durkheim (1912) concerning spiritual phenomenon: "The human mind has no need of properly scientific education to notice that there are definite sequences and a constant order of succession between phenomena *or to notice that this order is often disturbed.*" [italics mine] (p. 45). Most of us can agree with Webster's definition of religious, or religion: 'A set of beliefs concerning the nature and purpose of the universe, esp. when considered as the creation of a superhuman agency.'

Mysticism as defined by Webster is: "The doctrine of an immediate spiritual intuition of truths, or of a direct, intimate union of the soul with God through contemplation or spiritual ecstasy." Here again we have an ambiguity between spiritual and mystical. Here is Scholem (1960) concerning mysticism, who asks:

> Why does a Christian mystic always see Christian visions and not those of a Buddhist? Why does a Buddhist see the figures of his own pantheon and not Jesus or the Madonna? Why does a Kabbalist on his way to enlightenment meet the prophet Elijah and not some figure from an alien world? The answer, of course, is that the expression of their experience is immediately transposed into symbols from their own world, even if the objects of this experience are essentially the same and not, as some students of mysticism (p. 15).

James (1901) explains that "the words 'mysticism' and 'mystical' are often used as terms of mere reproach, to throw at any opinion which we regard as vague and vast and sentimental, and without a base in either facts or logic (p. 318)." So, I am not inclined to use the definitions of others, there are too many, and they're too ambiguous.

Everything just discussed and defined concerning spiritual, religious, or mystical is really phenomenology, which is a philosophy or method of inquiry based on the premise that reality consists of objects and events as they are perceived or understood in human consciousness and not of anything independent of human consciousness.

I suggest that the following testimonies be considered from the presenters' own-world orientation and consciousness, which is that of the recovery movement. I will differentiate whether these disclosures are spiritual awakenings, spiritual experiences, religious experiences, or mystical experiences.

Spiritual experiences; will consist of synchronicities (unlikely but meaningful coincidences) and other phenomenon that do not include religion or God.

Spiritual awakenings; will be that of the educational variety or a realization, and not including religion or God.

Religious experiences; always have an element of religion or God.

A mystical experience; will consist of experiences that *include* some kind of dialogue or interaction with a higher power, together with a usually radical or other-worldly phenomenon. A mystical category can also be indistinct or nebulous.

Keep in mind, however, in the real world—especially around 12-step meetings, the terms *spiritual awakening* and *spiritual experience* are interchangeable. I found that there was such a variety of experiences that I was inclined to separate them for this research study.

Having differentiated between terms, here is an account of Bill Wilson's (1984) "mystical" spiritual experience:*

> In his helplessness and desperation, Bill cried out, 'I'll do anything, anything at all!' He had reached a point of total, utter deflation—a state of complete, absolute surrender. With neither faith nor hope, he cried, 'If there be a God, let Him show Himself!' What happened next was electric. 'Suddenly, my room blazed with an indescribably white light. I was seized with an ecstasy beyond description. Every joy I had known was pale by comparison. The light, the ecstasy—I was conscious of nothing else for a time (pp. 120,121).

The following experiences, including the preceding one, are what Jung considered to be spiritual experiences.

Jim:

My friend Jim said, "It was not so much a spiritual experience, but a realization that there had to be some kind of change in order for me to go on living." He said that this took place when he took a trip to Death Valley. He wanted to take the tour at *Scotty's Castle* but he also needed a drink, so only having money to do one or the other, he "bought a

---

* Bill Wilson was cofounder of Alcoholic's Anonymous

bottle and walked up to Death Valley Scotty's grave and sat there and talked to a dead man for almost two hours." Then he told Scotty what he wanted his life to be like, asking him what he should do to achieve this. When Jim walked away from the grave, he had made a decision to change. What makes this a spiritual experience for Jim, is that he remembers he once told himself, "I'll get clean when hell freezes over." Ironically, it was snowing in Death Valley—the lowest elevation in the United States and a place that hardly ever sees snow. He had to take a circuitous route home because he was snowed in. Jim had a symbolic experience of hell freezing over in Death Valley. He said, "it was like a sign to me." Jim had a spiritual awakening that was characterized by a meaningful coincidence, and he has been an ardent member of NA since.

Stan:

This young man stopped in Barstow for a meeting on his way to Alabama. I had asked the group to speak on spiritual experience. When it was Stan's turn, he explained that when he was at his lowest, "drinking every day, drinking vodka for breakfast, and after two unsuccessful suicide attempts, I still did not have any realization about God. I could not come to believe." Being very close to his grandmother until she passed away, he prayed to *her* rather than God. In desperation while in a blackout, he said that "she appeared to me," and he asked her: "How do I go on living life, Grandma?" Her reply was: "Service to other people." Stan said "I don't know whether that was an alcoholic hallucination or a spiritual experience, but it opened my eyes, and I have since been of service to other people in the program." Though he did mention God, his experience was with the spirit of his deceased grandmother. Stan, the way I see it, had a spiritual experience.

Larry:

Some of the stories generated here as spiritual experiences are similar to some experiences written about by William James in *The Varieties of Religious Experience*. This holds true with Larry. His experience happened right after an argument with his wife. Driving into Barstow from his family's rural home, Larry reports having, "the most profound feeling of love I have ever had. It was not just for a couple seconds either. It lasted for a long time. As I was driving, this energy was generating out of myself and my truck. It was unbelievable." Larry said that he had never, before or since, experienced anything like it. Larry's paroxysm is common in the celestial sphere of spiritual experiences.

William James (1901) said "it may come gradually, or it may occur abruptly; it may come through altered feelings, or through altered powers of action; or it may come through new intellectual insights." James also explained;

> To find religion is only one out of many ways of reaching unity; and the process of remedying inner incompleteness and reducing inner discord is a general psychological process, which may take place with any sort of mental material, and need not necessarily assume the religious form. For example, the new birth may be away from religion into incredulity; or it may be from moral scrupulosity into freedom and license; or it may be produced by the irruption into the individual's life of some new stimulus or passion, such as *love*, [Larry's experience] ambition, cupidity, revenge, or patriotic devotion. In all these instances we have precisely the same psychological form of event—a firmness, stability, and equilibrium succeeding a period of storm and stress and inconsistency [Larry's quarrel with his wife] (p. 159).

Larry and I agree that he had a spiritual experience.

Terry:

This woman's experience was different. It happened gradually over a period of roughly two years. It started when the dysfunctional relationship she was in ended. Though she continued to use drugs, she was still having an ongoing experience. She sent her experience to me by email. I will quote it in its entirety:

> The part of the whole experience that really impressed me as being "miraculous" was the recovery process that went on, unbeknownst to me for the two years between "turning it over" and first walking through the doors of AA. The totality of events are too lengthy to include, but the fact that I had literally done every step in the program before I had ever seen them, seems like way more than a coincidence.

> The depression, desperation, and realization that "it wasn't working" was the First Step: "I realized that I was powerless over my addiction and that my life had become unmanageable."

The preceding years of spiritual studies had led up to Step Two: "I came to believe that a power greater than myself could restore me to sanity." This was like a split-second thing that almost immediately segued into Step Three: "I made the decision to turn my will and life over to the care of God as I understood Him." The talk I had with God (this was a real discussion, by the way), was the beginning of this step for me, walking out the door was the culmination of it.

The Fourth Step: "To make a searching and fearless moral inventory of ourselves" was an ongoing process that spanned the entire two years. I looked at every inch, every nook, every cranny of what made up "me". I didn't like what I saw very much. Then I started writing down all the things about me that I knew—the good stuff, the bad stuff. The childhood and adolescent shit that you don't tell anybody. How I felt about it. What I thought was real, what I thought was imagined, and how all of those experiences, real or perceived, were affecting me. It was, I suppose, an extended attempt at self-analyzation.

Step Five: "Admit to God, to ourselves, and to another human being the exact nature of our wrongs" was another drawn out process. The "other human being" was any MF who would listen to me. I was on a Mission. I wanted everybody I knew to know just exactly what a rotten, no-good, person I had become and why. I was really tired of hiding things. And I really had a "burning desire" to help other people not to make the same mistakes or to feel like they were the only "bad guys in town."

Step Six: "I became willing to have God remove all these defects of character." Well, duh...

Step Seven: "I humbly asked God to remove my shortcomings." This I did, also. Probably several times. I'm still doing this step today.

Step Eight: "To make a list of all the persons that we had harmed, and became willing to make amends to them all." I don't know that I listed "all" the people, but I did list many of them, including what I had done to hurt them.

Step Nine: "To make direct amends wherever possible" was just the natural outgrowth of having made the list in the first place, so I started doing that whenever I had the chance.

Step Ten: "I continued to take personal inventory and when I was wrong, promptly admitted it." Again, this was just a natural extension of Step Four, and I was still on that Mission.

Step Eleven: "Sought through prayer and meditation to improve my conscious contact with God as I understand Him." He IS my life, was then, is now.

Step Twelve: "Having had a spiritual awakening as a result of these steps, I tried to carry this message to addicts, and to practice these principles in all my affairs." Absolutely—I was still on my mission. I had developed "rigorous honesty" to a fault. I was out to save the world, and share this miraculous spiritual gift I had been given.

Maybe my story doesn't have the allure of "bright lights" and spectral visitation, but it is the truth, and it has forever changed my life.

Terry's experience is difficult to categorize. But early in her message she made the statement, "The talk I had with God (this was a real discussion, by the way), was the beginning of this step for me, walking out the door was the culmination of it." Having that one small element of God in comparison to the entire experience places Terry's experience in the category of spiritual experience, mainly because of its profound synchronicity. Synchronicity was defined by Jung as an acausal connecting principle, an essentially mysterious connection between the personal psyche and the material worked, based on the fact that at bottom they are only different forms of energy.

Cheryl:

After breaking up with her husband, Cheryl moved in with her mom in San Diego. She had been drinking heavily. Cheryl and her mom often had violent quarrels after being around each other for awhile; therefore, she started looking for her own apartment. When she had collected an entire page of phone numbers and addresses, she started making calls. When she was "about half way down the page, I dialed a number, and the person on the other end said '*Alcoholic's Anonymous.*' I was really shocked, and I hung the phone up. It was a wrong number—I just knew it was."

A couple of weeks later, Cheryl's husband came for a visit. He seemed so clean and calm, and Cheryl wanted to know how he did it?

She explained to him that she had been acting "real crazy", and he told her to go to AA.

Cheryl continues; "I thought, 'wow,' maybe I should go—because he'd been clean for about nine months. He looked so clean and calm. He had something that I wanted to have. I was drinking a lot of wine and being really crazy, and fighting with everybody." After her husband left, Cheryl started thinking: "I wonder if this could really be it." Then she started looking for that paper with all the numbers on it. "I found it and I talked to this guy. He told me that it sounds like your life is unmanageable." At this point Cheryl laughed and said, "Today I know what that means, but then I thought 'how does that guy know— how does he know my life is unmanageable?" She started going to meetings, and about two weeks later she wondered how this happened, "So I went back to where I wrote that number down, and when I looked at the paper, I had switched two numbers. So, looking for an apartment and switching those two numbers because I'm dyslexic, I found *Alcoholic's Anonymous.*" Cheryl was sober sixteen years when I interviewed her. Another spiritual experience, not because of a coincidence, but because of a mistake.

Harold:

My friend Harold's experience is what would be considered by many as religious, and I must agree. Abstinent from the use of any chemical substances for approximately sixty days, Harold was "incapable of eating, was bleeding internally, vomiting and crapping blood, and having nose bleeds for sixteen days. I had lost a lot of weight." He had also been breaking out with sores caused from herpes, which he had for some time. Harold left an AA meeting and went to a friend's apartment. At this point he was experiencing incomprehensible demoralization: "Crying, hurting, and had had enough, and feeling like I was going to die." He said that he lied down on the floor and looked up and said, "Fuck it; fuck it God, help me. Please, if there's anything there either heal me or kill me. I can't take it anymore." He then said with emphasis "that no sooner had 'more' come out of my mouth, a light hit me and encompassed my whole body, and I was immediately raised above my body with still full control of my senses. I could hear my body behind me crying—whimpering. It was inside of this light. It was just this overwhelming sense of peace and ease. It was a place that I've never been able to get into words." The only thing that Harold's doppelganger experience could compare to, he said, "was that of a hundred thousand orgasms. As I was above my body, this wind and light kind of blew through me, and at that moment I knew that I would never have to use drugs or drink alcohol again. I actually heard a voice saying that I was healed, and that if I ever had the opportunity to tell this story, to tell it." He then explained the process of coming back into his body with the light, wind and sensations disappearing into a halcyon of inner peace. After that, Harold said, "the way I could see was different, everything around me seemed to be glowing. It seemed like I could actually see the atomic structure of air for a few moments, then the very next thought was that I flipped out." Then his overwhelming experience was over and he went to sleep. When he awoke the next morning, he remembered the experience, and acknowledged that he still felt different, and had no desire for drugs and alcohol. The most astonishing part of this story is that Harold was not bleeding anymore. Also, from that day on, he has not suffered any symptoms from herpes. He suffered monthly sores and lesions from herpes from 1986 until this happened in 1990, and since then there is not a trace after having gotten biyearly checkups for at least two years. Harold had what I consider a religious experience because what he went through had elements that *included* some kind of dialogue or interaction with God, but the more extraordinary element was that it also consisted of a radical other-worldly phenomenon, which could arguably be placed in the mystical category.

Michele:

Here is another one that was emailed to me. Michele is a woman who I used to drink and use with in Barstow. Her story is quoted in its entirety from Las Cruces, New Mexico:

> When I first moved here to get sober I didn't have much money and no friends. Thanksgiving was here and I wanted to go to the Arid Club [an AA club] to eat a free turkey dinner. I had saved two Kennedy silver half dollars from all my drugging in Barstow, because I loved Kennedy. I had enough gas in the truck to get to the club but I didn't have enough to get home. I figured God would surely want me to spend Thanksgiving with other people and eat good, but what about the gas? I prayed and asked God to give me the gas money home from the club. But, just in case I took my Kennedy half dollars. I only needed a dollars worth of gas. Anyway, I got to the club and sat in a chair watching all the people mill about. Every time someone would pass by me, I would think "there goes a dollar." I told myself not to ask anyone, to wait for God to supply my need. I sat there for about twenty minutes when

this guy came over to me and asked me if I needed any money. My mouth fell open and I looked up and smiled. I told this man yes, I did need money. He gave me a dollar twenty-five. By waiting twenty minutes I got 25 cents more than I would have asked for myself. This particular incident has caused me to believe, and when I get in doubt these days, I can recall the miracle. Some years later I was sharing about this incident in a meeting and this woman found it touching. Every year on my sobriety date she gave me another Kennedy half dollar.

Michele having included God in her disclosure, places it in the religious experience category. Some experiences are graced with bright lights and celestial voices, but experiences on the opposite end of the spectrum can be just as meaningful to those who had them.

Tom:

Tom and a fellow AA member responded to a 12-step call. They tried getting the man into a treatment facility from Covina to Corona to San Bernardino. They were left with only one more place to go in Upland. "It so happened that this was Dennis Kneivel—Evel Kneivel's brother. They had two locked doors at this hospital, and somehow we walked right through them. We were standing by the cubicle where the nurses were. They turned around and said, 'there is no way you guys could have walked through those doors. How did you get in here?' We just explained to her that we just opened the door and walked in, and that it was the last place we had to go. They wouldn't believe us at first. They looked around and there wasn't anybody else there but us." Fortunately, they admitted Dennis into the hospital. Tom said "I do not know how long he stayed sober or what, it makes no difference, but that was a major spiritual experience in my life." Evidently the lock mechanism couldn't be opened from the outside with a key, and there were only a couple of people there close enough and they didn't open it from the inside. Spiritual experiences consist of synchronicities (unlikely but meaningful coincidences) and other phenomenon that do not include religion or God. I believe Tom placed it in the appropriate category.

Mike:

Mike shared with me; "It was my second night out of detox at BMC. As I was trying to sleep, and I was going over in my head how I was going to 'trick' the system again so I could continue living the way I was accustomed—ie, drinking a twelve-pack every night at least." Mike had already said his usual prayers; "I've always done that—as well as a couple of new ones they taught me at BMC. Then, all of a sudden, there was like a bright light in my head and a voice that wasn't mine talking to me (ie, outside of me) that said, 'Trust me. With me you can do it one day at a time." Mike said that as soon as it had come, it was gone, and then he asked himself, "What was that?" Upon realizing it was not "my thinking," he thought maybe these AA people had something about how a higher power could help him, "and how I can't do it alone, cause that's what I was thinking when it happened—how I was gonna get myself through this one." Since then his cravings are gone and he has not had the desire to drink or use again. That was eight years prior to this interview. Did Mike have a mystical, religious, or a spiritual experience? Since he didn't specifically mention religion or God, I place it with the spiritual experiences.

Jackie:

Jackie's son was in the hospital. He had been clean and sober about two years but his recovery was tenuous. Before leaving the hospital during a visit, little Jack asked his dad: "Am I going to have to worry about you drinking and using now?" Jackie assured him that he had no need to worry. How confident he was inside with how he answered his son's question, was also tenuous. However, Jackie's confidence was solidified when his son passed away a week later. What could be worse than losing a son or daughter? Admittedly, Jackie would have probably lost his sobriety date had his son not died. The reason Jackie considers this a spiritual experience, and I agree, is that his recovery would not have been sustained if he had not assured little Jack otherwise.

Gina:

Gina's opprobrium had been disappointing her two kids for years, and she would not come to terms with the humiliation she found herself in resulting from her addiction. She went to treatment *again*. After she was there for a while, it somehow occurred to her that she was admitted to the rehab on her son's birthday: What a revelation! She had many previous sobriety dates, some from rehabs and some from NA, but this one was special. After being released after six and a half months, she held onto her recovery, sometimes by just a thread. That thread was her clean date. She said that her recovery probably would not have lasted had she not had this supposed "coincidence" to hang on to. Like Jackie,

Gina had a spiritual experience, contingent on the love of a son, that kept her clean and sober after disappointing her kids so many times before.

Up to this time the experiences I have collected have been in some way related to their recovery from addiction. The following experience is from an AA member, but the experience is not connected to his drinking and subsequent recovery. I don't remember for sure, but I might have neglected to inform him beforehand that I was collecting experiences that were connected in some way to recovery. Or, I might have just wanted to include it because it was so inexplicable.

Gilbert:

This man, who was in his seventies at the time, told me that he was driving a truck up a mountain for his employer. The truck broke down, and it was getting dark. He said that he "could hear the birds and the wind, and see the trees and the stars in the sky. It was a beautiful night, you know." There wasn't much traffic, so Gilbert asked himself, "What am I going to do? So I decided to pray. 'God,' I said, 'I know that you exist, I know you're real, that you're taking care of me, and I know you made the heavens and everything that is here. I am alone here. If you would, do something to let me know you're really here." After praying, he looked out of the truck window at the stars, but focused on only one. He stared at the one star for a while, then noticed "that it was getting closer." The closer the star got, the brighter everything around him was getting, especially illuminating "the whole truck." He said, "What is happening to me? It's getting closer and brighter." Being confused—not scared he told me, he got on the floorboard. By the time he looked up, "it was only about ten feet away. It was so bright that it was like being inside of a lightbulb—even brighter, so bright that it was blinding me." Nothing more happened while the star was still there, but after it left, "I noticed something: I couldn't hear the birds or the wind no more. The whole world stood still. Not a sound. Then I realized that God was showing me what I had asked of him." Gilbert's religious experience was mystical.

Before I conclude the experiences, I want to establish a common thread that goes through a majority of them. Remember Larry, who said "I had the most profound feeling of love I ever had."And Harold, the one who left his body? Mike, who heard a voice that wasn't his own? And then Gilbert who experienced the bright light when his truck broke down. Also, there's...

Leah:

She shared with me that when her life was totally out of control at six years sober she put off getting a bottle till the next day, and that night in bed she had an overwhelming sense of peace and warmth, accompanied with an inner assurance that she would not ever have to drink or use again.

Pat:

As he was driving home one afternoon, he "was passing an old barn on top of a hill overlooking a valley below. Suddenly, the colors of the day and the pastoral scene became vivid. There was a feeling of a tuning fork being struck. The vibrations seemed to fill all my senses and for the first time in a long time, I realized I was alive and a party to the beauty around me. This all happened in an instant but my memory of this is vivid with the ability to recall the scene and the vibration at anytime. It seemed to be a coming in tune with the universe."

Lawrence:

He told me about sitting on his bed when a bright light and a warm feeling came over him. His experience was brief but profound, one that he said he would never forget.

*   *   *

The most common thread running through most of these *spiritual* experiences are the feelings of peace, warmth, love, etc., also bright lights of varying degrees and kinds, and of 'voices' (which were not always with God necessarily). The rest of them were not as relative, but definitely unique and fascinating.

My previous ignorance concerning spiritual experience has transformed into more of an understanding than I was asking for. I have realized that spiritual awakening, and religious and mystical experiences, can be thought of under the umbrella term—spiritual experience. However, one can also isolate spiritual experience in any way they choose without using the terminology or the defined categories I have presented here. A good example would be Gina, who went into treatment on her son's birthday. A more common description of Gina's spiritual experience would be a simple coincidence.

Considering Gina's experience as spiritual has enabled me to realize that I have also had a similar spiritual experience; however, until this data collection, I never thought of it as that.

About nine months after my release from prison, I was visiting my daughter and her husband. We were talking about sobriety dates. I mentioned that mine was May 7th. She looked at me and said, "I really haven't put much emphasis on my sobriety date, but that date rings a bell." She dug around in some drawers and came out with a piece of paper with the same sobriety date on it! We shared the warmth of the moment and each of us carried the information in our respective ways. I have stayed clean and sober, but I might have anyway, and maybe that's why I didn't consider it a "spiritual experience"—perhaps more of a significant awakening. Since it's possible that it helped sustain my recovery, at least for a period of time, I simply refer to it now as a spiritual experience.

Having categorized the previous disclosures as spiritual experiences, spiritual awakenings, religious experiences, and mystical experiences, I wondered during my research if one could have all of them at once. Bucke (1969), in a work originally published in 1901, describes an experience that could be thought of that way:

> He was in a state of quiet, almost passive enjoyment. All at once, without warning of any kind, he found himself wrapped around as it were by a flame-colored cloud. For an instant he thought of fire, some sudden conflagration in the great city; the next, he knew that the light was within himself. Directly afterwards came upon him a sense of exultation, of immense joyousness accompanied or immediately followed by an intellectual illumination quite impossible to describe. Into his brain streamed one momentary lightning-flash of the Brahmic Splendor which has ever since lightened his life; upon his heart fell one drop of Brahmic Bliss, leaving thenceforward for always an aftertaste of heaven. Among other things he did not come to believe, he saw and knew that the Cosmos is not dead matter but a living Presence, that the soul of man is immortal, that the universe is so built and ordered that without any peradventure all things work together for the good of each and all, that the foundation principle of the world is what we call love and that the happiness of every one is in the long run absolutely certain. He claims that he learned more within the few seconds during which the illumination lasted than in previous months or even years of study, and that he learned much that no study could ever have taught (p. 10).

During the collection of data, I have come to realize that my project was limited. The scope of the spiritual experiences I collected were limited to the confines of recovered addicts and alcoholics. I am also aware that the scope of spiritual experiences are probably limited. For example, the religious denominations and the multitude of people within them, undoubtedly have many variations of religious experiences—not to mention many other kinds of mystical experiences. Also, the sample population that contributed to my project is also limited in ways: geography, nationality or ethnicity—cultural differences within those groups, religious and educational backgrounds. I will not elaborate further on the many ways my research was limited; however, regardless of its limitations, I believe I have answered my original question: what is a spiritual experience?

But most important, how has my research contributed to the *anima mundi* (the soul of the world)? How, after several years of attendance at 12-step meetings, I could *not* have had the knowledge, or a working definition of spiritual experience, I can only speculate. And if this were the case with me, how many others attending 12-step meetings are just as ignorant? Whereas my ignorance did not cause me to return to active addiction, it could have. What if Gina had not noticed the supposed coincidence of being admitted into treatment on her son's birthday? She told me what would have happened, as it had so many times before. Would Jackie have stayed clean if his dying son had not asked him if he had to worry about his dad drinking and using anymore? Jackie knows the answer to that question. I have only touched on some of the experiences that have been conducive to recovery for many; therefore, if those who attend meetings make it a point to explain to newcomers the nature and importance of spiritual experiences, maybe they will be able to recognize them when they happen. Newcomers have a lot on their minds, and having spiritual experiences could well sound quite ridiculous in early recovery unless it can be explained in a way that is palatable to them.

My present life would not be as abstemious as it is had I not, for purely selfish reasons, volunteered for a substance abuse education program when I was in prison. Who could have told a philistine like me that a prison sentence would be the best thing that would happen to me in my entire life?

CHAPTER 10

THINKING OUR WAY
TO GOOD LIVING

C riminalized drug addicts don't think like normal people; therefore, let's explore their thinking so normies can get more of an understanding of how they think, and so jointsters themselves can learn why they need to monitor and discipline their thought processes.

Directed thinking is purposeful, reasoned and goal directed—it is thought and knowledge, and the relationship between them. The ability to plan, have flexibility, be persistent, and have the willingness to self-correct are the characteristics of directed thinking essential for the recovering addict to learn.

Directed thinking cannot be spontaneous; we don't get up in the morning and think our way through brushing our teeth, because we do that by second nature or habit. Recovering addicts and alcoholics bring many of their old behaviors into recovery with them, and spontaneity, in the form of hasty decisions, is commonplace. Directed thinking involves the use of various cognitive functions, one of which is memory.

MEMORY

A good definition for memory is the recall of the past which involves learning; however, Random House Webster's dictionary defines it as: "The faculty or process of retaining or recalling past experiences."

There are many mnemonic devices to aid memory, and most jointsters will concede that they lost a portion of that ability that was previously available to them. Acrostics are sentences created by words that begin with the first letters of a series of words. For example, "Every good boy does fine," is the music student's acrostic for recalling the

notes associated with the lines of a treble clef staff; EGBDF. Another
one—one that normies might use when balking about drug addicts
moving into or living in their neighborhood—is NIMBY (not in my
back yard). Rhymes and songs like the McDonald's song, "Nobody can
do it like (you-know-who) can." Or how about, "Twidle-lee dee, twidle-
lee dum, gimmy your dope or I'll get my gun." The loci system is a
good one, which uses visual associations with locations you already
know. The peg system is another, it employs key words represented by
numbers. For example; one is a bun, two is a shoe, three is a tree. The
phonetic system is similar to the peg system, but instead of words
representing numbers, sounds represent numbers. If recovering
jontsters would employ some of these methods, they would inevitably
improve their memories; however, unlearning long ingrained habits is
difficult to do, especially when there is no incentive to do it. Jointsters
are often discriminated against, which is why they will think such
things as, "Why even try? What good will it do?"

What we usually refer to as forgetting, is either the inability to
recall stored information or the failure to store information in the first
place. Recovering addicts, especially the practicing ones, have what I
call selective memory syndrome—that is, the failure to store
information in the first place. The addict's attitude is—if the
information isn't of any immediate use, then why make the effort to
remember it?

Lucas (1990) explains a memory technique that he invented when
he was a kid. He said that when he went places with his parents in the
car, one of the ways he would spend time burning up excess energy was
to look at signs along the highway; for example, he saw an oil company
sign that read SHELL, then he wondered to himself what that word
would look like in alphabetical order, and he came up with EHLLS (p
xi). There's no specific purpose for this example, but it's a good way
for jointsters, or anybody for that matter, to exercise their brain. The
brain is a muscle, and our muscles need to be exercised.

Psychologist Gordon Allport showed research participants a picture
of a white man with a knife holding up a black man with a suit. This
picture was presented in a flash to test the accuracy of their eyewitness
testimony in a situation in which racial prejudice might influence their
perception. How our memory can be influenced by biases, prejudices,
and stereotypes should lead us to question ourselves periodically. The
same scenario, of course, could be substituted with a man in a suit
holding up a younger man with facial hair, long scraggly hair or a bald
head, with tatoos on his arms and neck—the stereotypical jointster.

Xenophobia and discrimination isn't restricted to ethnic groups, jointsters often deal with it in diverse ways. I know I do.

REASONING

Revlin and Mayer (1978) tell us;

> As people, we don't use the same psychological processes in finding conclusions required by the laws of formal logic or reasoning. Biases, prejudices and our emotions are some reasons why we're unable to do this. The notion of an irrational reasoner has been given reviewed interest as a result of the acceptance of categorical syllogisms into the social psychological literature as a diagnostic metric for assessing attitudes and beliefs. It is a frequent conclusion of such research with categorical syllogisms that the untrained reasoners are not strictly logical in their inferences and that they base their decisions primarily on personal knowledge and biases (p. 52).

Normies will base their decisions and their *observations* primarily on personal knowledge and biases when associating drug use with appearances. Jointsters can usually identify other jointsters, and not from the stereotypical observations such as shaved heads, tatoos, long hair, and/or their attire—anybody can do that. I'm talking about a look, a very subtle one that's in their countenance, their walk—the way they carry themselves. All the other stereotypical nuances may not be there, but a Jointster can *generally* recognize a fellow jointster without those nuances being present.

Jointsters are very adept at manipulation and persuasion; therefore, most of them don't believe they can be bamboozled (ya can't con a con). They're wrong about that because they're basing their decisions primarily on personal knowledge and biases. They doubt that the man with the 'normie' appearance is capable of hoodwinking them, and you'll rarely hear them admit it when it happens. Let's have a look at four different types of reasoning given to us by Halpern (1989):

1. Inductive reasoning - If I have a situation where a statement has two premises, and the premises are logical, then I can find a valid conclusion through inductive reasoning (p. 126).

Here's a superficial example: If every person I have ever seen is a jointster, I would use this evidence to support the conclusion that everyone in the world is a jointster. Obviously I can't be absolutely positive of this fact. It's always possible that someone who I've never met is not a jointster. However if I met just one person that wasn't a jointster, then my conclusion must be wrong. So it is with inductive reasoning. I can never prove that my conclusion is correct, but I can disprove it. Jointsters often have a difficult time with inductive reasoning when it comes to dealing with people. When dealing with normies in the real world, they will often employ the same strategies or tactics that they have been using with people like themselves. And when they try to *not* do that, they end up under or overestimating who they're dealing with, or they make an enemy, or they're ignored, etc.

2. Deductive reasoning - With this type of reasoning, you would begin with statements known or believed to be true (p. 128).

A simple example would be the statement, "all jointsters use drugs," then you could conclude that Lynda, a woman you've never met, also uses drugs. This is the *modus operandi* of most people, including jointsters, but jointsters can carry it too far. For example, if I believe all jointsters are thieves, then to me it isn't being unethical to steal from other jointsters. As I mentioned throughout this book, jointsters need to continually monitor and discipline their thought processes.

3. Syllogistic reasoning - In a nutshell, this form of reasoning is deciding whether a conclusion can properly be inferred from two or more statements. One type of syllogistic reasoning is categorical reasoning, which involves terms that tell us how many, like 'some,' 'none,' and 'no' (p. 128).

There are several types of syllogistic reasoning, which can quickly get recondite and technical; therefore, I'll just expand on the type cited above. I have made an effort in this work to use terminology such as 'some, often, many, or most,' when referring to pre-criminalized addicts or jointsters. I can't say with assurance that all jointsters are thieves or that all addicts are *puerile*. I have tried to deal with majorities in my examples, and if I haven't been consistent during this work, then read it again and replace my error with language that's more accurate. Anyway, this is something that I've had to learn to do. Prior to recovery, which is *common* with jointsters (notice I didn't say with *all* jointsters), I made blanket statements. Blanket statements are *often* prejudicial statements, and I don't mean racial prejudice. Prejudice means to pre-judge, and many people prejudge jointsters by labeling them.

4. Probabilistic reasoning - is using information where we have to decide whether a conclusion is likely true—or not likely true. In everyday contexts, much of our reasoning is probabilistic (p. 163).

Suppose I learn that people who have hepatitis C are frequently nauseous, depressed, and are lacking in energy. I then notice that I have these same symptoms. Does that mean that I have hep C? It shouldn't, because those symptoms can be caused by other conditions and/or circumstances. However, when former intravenous drug users have these symptoms, then they should assume they have hep C, or at least get tested for it. Given this example, it's easy enough to see how jointsters could mistakenly come to conclusions based on their addictive mind-set and lifestyle.

According to Halpern, "Much of our thinking is like the scientific method of hypothesis testing. A hypothesis is a set of beliefs about the nature of the world; it is usually a belief about a relationship between two or more variables" (p. 223). There are several methods of testing hypotheses including: inductive and deductive methods; through operational definitions; independent and dependent variables; measurement sensitivity; populations and samples; and variability. Furthermore, there are several ways to determine cause: isolation and control of variables; prospective and retrospective research; correlation and cause (which people frequently get confused); illusory correlation; validity; and reliability. I've learned to be aware of self-fulfilling prophecies in life as well as learning to think in a directed manner. For the most part, I accept the effectiveness of double-blind studies, depending on the merits of the research sample. In my previous life when I wrote and called in my own medical prescriptions, I became familiar with double-blind studies while researching pharmaceutical drugs for my personal use. Through a double-blind study I learned that propoxyphene (Darvon) is less effective for pain than plain Aspirin. However, when I wanted to detox for a while, I also learned that propoxyphene was effective for treating withdrawal symptoms resulting from the physical addiction to opiates.

DECISION MAKING

Decision-making can be stressful, and it isn't limited to the uneducated: Whenever there is a simple error that most lay people fall for, there is always a slightly more sophisticated version of the same problem that experts also fall for. I didn't write scrips only for mind altering substances. I utilized my scam to provide prescription medication for my family. Obviously, a physician's expertise through experience would enable him to select more appropriate drugs than I did, even though I had a working knowledge of the Physician's Desk Reference. But I did it anyway, and luckily didn't do any harm to myself or my family. My decision to treat family members with drugs that I wrote scrips for could have been disastrous if there were medical issues involved that I was unaware of.

Halpern remarks that the availability heuristic is a rule of thumb we use to solve problems (p.314). For example, when I read the question about whether there were more deaths due to homicide or due to diabetes-related diseases, and then read the answer (diabetes) and the reason why (the media), something clicked in my head. I'm now more aware of the effects of publicity. The media being in our face so much with all the murder and mayhem being publicized, naturally homicide was my choice. I was also fascinated that the availability of information in our memory will frequently determine the alternative selected in a decision-making process.

In early recovery, we need to go to meetings—a lot of them. When meeting time rolls around, sometimes we're faced with a decision—to go or not to go. Let's say the meeting I attended last night wasn't a very good one, but the availability of information in my memory from today concerns a money-making scheme. The alternative I select stands a good chance of being the one for making money, even though I may not need money as much as what I might learn in a meeting to enhance and sustain my recovery.

Many common myths inhibit recovering addicts from taking the essential steps for sound decision making. Let's explore some.

The future is a matter of chance or luck, so there's no use spending a lot of time and effort trying to make the best possible decision about something that isn't really significant.

Is this not uncommon jointster thinking? Also, as I mentioned before, we bring a lot of our old thinking patterns into recovery with us, which contributes to high relapse rates. In the face of discrimination, we cannot make such blanket statements as, what's the use of pursuing an education if nobody will have anything to do with ex-cons? The discrimination that I've encountered with trying to teach in colleges and universities concerning my criminal background has not in any way given me cause to regret my education. Many older jointsters say such things as, "I'm too old to go to school." That's balderdash! Let's say she is 40 years old. In four years she will be 44 years old, whether she gets a bachelors degree or not. Which is better, 44 years old with or without a bachelors degree?

Asking questions about an opportunity is asking for trouble.

This myth sounds rather ridiculous; however, especially in early recovery, our thinking is muddled and we're often overwhelmed. It's like the student who is afraid to ask a question because he or she is afraid it will be thought of as a stupid question. Perhaps we can all learn this lesson from a four year old boy. When I was a kid, my mom was babysitting the little brother of one of my friends. My mom was busy writing a letter or something, when she heard a racket in the kitchen. When she entered the kitchen, there sat the little guy with everything that was in the lower cupboards spread all over the floor. "Danny, you're not supposed to get into other people's things. It isn't nice!" Little Danny looked up at her in earnest and said, "How me supposed to know what you got if me no look?"

Experts always agree. If you've asked one, you've asked them all.

Along with other character flaws, jointsters bring sloth into early recovery with them, so wouldn't it make sense to take the time and effort to do the research, rather than taking the word of one expert? Recovering jointsters aren't the only ones who can benefit from deflating this myth. Most adjunct (part time) college instructors are professionals of some kind. Many of these instructors are also educated know-it-alls. I call the educated know-it-all 'the sage on the stage.' They'll stand up there and spew out information like it was indisputable, and much of their *performance* is an egotistical and arrogant need to bolster their self-importance. What they do is spew their opinions as facts along with legitimate facts. I use educators as examples because I witnessed this in academia. So yes, deflate this myth and get a second or third opinion.

   Now let's turn this around onto recovering jointsters. The prisons are full of jailhouse lawyers—some deservedly, but most not. The knowledge that these jointsters profess to know is usually just as egotistical and arrogant as the sage on the stage. They're not only jailhouse lawyers, but they're jailhouse psychologists, sociologists, anthropologists, and every other 'ists' that you can think of, and they bring all of that with them when they hit the streets. *Understanding* the lived experiences of these people is fraught with paradox, ambivalence, contradiction, and uncertainty. Therefore, we have personalities with inflated egos who often think of themselves as scumbag sewer rats. Some consciously feel about themselves in this way, which translates into diminished self worth, or its unconscious, and then it usually manifests in behavior that will get them incarcerated again.

Consulting non-experts is pointless.

Who are you going to trust—a drug and alcohol counselor with one or two years of education who is a recovered addict, or a normie with a Ph.D. in clinical psychology? All that education that the Ph.D. has, is little comfort to the recovering addict. I'm not saying that normies with clinical degrees aren't qualified to do the job. I'm saying that recovering addicts are more comfortable with those who have a background similar to theirs.

Also, professionals who are enmeshed in their own fields of expertise are often hard pressed to look outside of the box of their discipline for innovative ideas. When looking for answers in their own discipline, it's often more productive to ask those who are far removed from that discipline for ideas or answers. A plumber might come up with an insight that the psychologist is overlooking because he or she is trapped inside of a mind-set.

If the members in your group of decision makers agree on the same choice without anyone dissenting, you can feel secure that it is a sound decision.

If it's a 12-step group, be aware that 12-step groups are not hot-beds of mental health—they're addicts who, like everybody else, make mistakes and periodically agree with each other. When I first started going to meetings after I was released from prison, there was a highly respected man with 30 years of sobriety who used to say, "you can't think your way to good living, you have to live your way to good thinking." I had been taught that we need to monitor and discipline our thoughts to change the way we live, which would equate to 'thinking your way to good living.' Well, a lot of people heard him say that it's better to 'live your way to good thinking,' and so it started getting parroted at meetings all over the area by others.

Sometimes we need to challenge the status quo. When teaching the few college courses that I did, I encouraged my students to challenge the status quo—challenge even what I said (but don't get carried away), and even challenge what's in the text books. That is how innovation occurs. If we operate on nothing but present knowledge, then we stagnate.

Commitments are always irrevocable.

Don't misunderstanding this one. As long as we're not making a *habit* of breaking commitments, which most of us were doing when we were out there doing our thing, it is okay to break commitments once in a while if we give plenty of notice. It's not okay to leave people hanging or call the last minute and cancel.

PROBLEM SOLVING

A tendency in problem-solving, especially with jointsters, is to pick the first solution that comes to mind and run with it. The disadvantage of this approach is that you may run off a cliff or into a worse problem than you started with. A better strategy in solving problems of course, is to select the most practical course from many ideas.

If I don't have a clue how to plan, then it wouldn't do me any good for someone to tell me to plan a solution. If I can't think of any solutions, then how am I going to generate and evaluate any? Halpern gives us strategies that can help generate solutions. All of them won't work for everybody, but learning how to use different strategies can give us direction for problem solving. However, some of these strategies don't lend themselves as solutions for recovering jointsters, but others are self-explanatory. I'll give some examples.

Means-Ends Analysis - When a goal is not immediately attainable, we often need to take detours to break the problem down into smaller problems, called subproblems, each with its own goal, called subgoals (p. 373).

Let's say that a concerned parent wants to help their son get out of the pits of addictive despair. This isn't an easy task, so the problem needs to be broken down into a smaller problem—say, learning about addiction first. To solve this subproblem it will be necessary to set a goal—learn about dealing with addicts by going to Ala-non or Nar-anon, and work from there.

Simplification - A good way to approach problems is to strip away as much of the complexity as possible to reduce it to a simple form (p. 377).

When jointsters attend groups, say in a drug rehab, they're bombarded with solutions, techniques, and strategies to help keep them in recovery when they leave. They are told that they only need to change one thing—everything—but that's not going to happen overnight, so the best way to proceed is incrementally. Implement change slowly—one step at a time, and make a conscious effort to avoid getting overwhelmed.

I worked in a drug rehab as a recovery advocate, also referred to as a 'counselor 1' at other facilities. I used to facilitate four different groups, one of which was nutrition. When I first started, I bombarded the clients with information because I was coming at them from an educator's perspective. I came to realize that information wasn't the only thing they needed. They also needed practical suggestions to use in the real world, so I started integrating suggestions along with the information, and I used my personal experience as a tool. Implementing change incrementally is exceptionally difficult for recovering jointsters, because, as I stated in Chapter Five, they want what they want now, or yesterday. Anyway, I suggested that they start with one thing, such as keeping their carbohydrates down to 75 grams per day at first, which would get them used to reading food labels. Get used to that, then eliminate or cut down considerably on sugar—mainly sweets like candy and bakery products, then switch from regular soda to diet, etc. Incremental change is possible with jointsters whereas radical change is not always realistic or practical.

Random Search and Trial-and-Error - A truly random search would mean that there is no systematic order to which possible solutions can be explored. A trial and error search is best applied to well-defined problems with few possible solution paths (p. 381).

A random search for addicts usually means grasping for straws, or drawing from the knowledge of jailhouse lawyers and psychologists, which isn't an option that recovering jointsters should take. However, a trial and error process is usually within their grasp. A lot of recovering addicts go back to school, but not all of them finish. Many addicts are attracted to the idea of going to college, but doesn't it make more sense to take one class first to test the waters, rather than going to all the trouble of applying (which in itself is time-consuming), filling out all those tedious financial aide forms, enrolling full time, and then finding out that it was all a big mistake to begin with—that you aren't cut out for it? However, I don't recommend trying this with drugs, which so many jointsters do. "Well, I just smoke pot and drink, and leave the meth alone. This trial and error process backfires repeatedly with DUIs, possession charges and a continued dependency on mind altering substances. In this area, jointsters need, absolutely have to have, radical change.

Rules - Some kinds of problems, like *series* problems, depend on rules. Once the underlying principles are established, the problem is solved (381).

My example is very simple. If I am continually going to jail (a *series* of events) for violating the law, then I need to stop violating the law. Of course, if the problem is drug and/or alcohol oriented, then the problem is compounded and the first rule would be to stop using the drugs and/or alcohol. On the surface this example seems superficial or obvious, but many of those who don't have any understanding whatever of the jointster population think it's as easy as simply not breaking the law, or stopping drinking or using. One of my friends' parents looked at me in earnest, and asked, "Why doesn't he just stop drinking?" I said, "Because he can't." He replied with, "Well you did it, why can't he?" Most people do not understand the dynamics of addiction, plus the fact that most people are unable to accomplish it on a permanent basis. Remember, the available recovery options don't work very well, but it's all we have.

Brainstorming - This one is fun—a method for group problem solving (p. 385).

This is one that I used in my groups at the rehab. It's not only fun, but it's effective. For example, in my group on 'change' I would ask the clients to brainstorm on the subject of triggers. Triggers, simply defined, are events that precipitates other events. All recovering addicts know what they are. If an alcoholic walks by a bar, he is inevitably going to be struck by the odors, which could serve as a trigger for a relapse. An intravenous drug addict watching someone fix in a movie could also trigger a relapse. Anger is a very common trigger, which is why it is suggested that addicts not get too hungry, angry, lonely, or tired (HALT—another acronym). This reminds me of another acronym—FINE, which is often used when someone asks, how are you doing?" The next time someone answers you with "fine," you might wonder if they're feeling Fucked up, Insecure, Neurotic, and Emotional.

Restating the Problem - This is a useful strategy for ill-defined problems. In well-defined problems, the goal is usually explicitly stated in unambiguous terms that leave little room for restatement (p. 386).

Recovering jointsters, or anyone else for that matter, often want to know how they can save money? They shop in discount markets, cut coupons out of the newspapers, cut back on gas, and spend their weekends at home rather than going out. Suppose the problem is restated so that it becomes, "How can I have more money?" Their solutions then change to such things as, getting a higher paying job or moving to where rent is cheaper. Asking the questions in different ways give us more options.

Analogies and Metaphors - Mythology and fairy tales have been assisting the human condition for hundreds of years (p. 387).

We can draw on alchemy for this one. The prima materia in the alchemical vessel has to be destroyed (killed) before the transformation process can start taking place. Think of the old jointster self (in the dregs of addiction) as the prima materia that has to be killed, and the new recovered self as the finished product; the philosophers stone; the individuation of the recovery process; the Gold.

CREATIVE THINKING

The notions of unusual or unique, and good or useful, is what is involved in creativity. It always involves judgement, and people may not agree on which actions or outcomes deserve to be labeled creative.

Not all creative people are alike either, which makes defining creativity a challenge and assessing it a monumental undertaking. The traditional psychological definition of creativity includes two parts: originality and functionality. You can't be creative unless you come up with something that hasn't been done before. The idea has to work, or be adaptive or be functional in some way; it has to meet some criteria of usefulness. There is a distinction to be made between creativity (lower case c) and Creativity (upper case C): creativity, which is often used as an indicator of mental health, includes everyday problem-solving and the ability to adapt to change. Creativity, on the other hand, is far more rare. It occurs when a person solves a problem or creates an object that has a major impact on how other people think, feel, and live their lives. Mere creativity implies basic functionality. Creativity is something for which we give Pulitzer and Nobel Prizes for.

I've chosen to end this book with an Afterword in the form of a story. I don't believe it's anything worthy of a Nobel, or even a Pulitzer Prize, but hopefully it will contribute to an *understanding* of criminalized drug addicted tricksters (jointsters).

Afterword

QUANTUM RECOVERY

According to Goswami (1995) "whenever we ask if there is some other kind of reality beyond material reality, we are putting material realism on the spot. Similarly, a genuine discontinuity points to a transcendent order of reality and thus a breakdown of material realism" (p. 138).

A quantum particle: (1) can be in two places at the same time, (2) doesn't exist until it is observed, (3) can go from one place to another without going through the intervening space, (4) can influence other particles at a distance.

I got off work at six o'clock in the evening, went home and sifted through my mail, listened to my phone messages, then went to a restaurant for dinner. As I was waiting in line to pay my bill, the man in front of me turned around to leave and we made eye contact. "Wow, is that really you?" We had not seen each other in 25 years. We stepped outside, and after a few minutes of small talk, he asked if I wanted to hang out for a while and catch up. I said yes. He told me that he was supposed to meet someone at a local bar, and his business would only take a little while.

Considering how long I had been clean and sober, I didn't think it would be too risky to go with him and chat for a while. *Nuncest bibendum*—now is the time to drink. Three hours later, after 10 years in recovery, we were still in the bar and I was well on my way to getting drunk. We also did some drugs together like we did so many years before. On my way home to sleep it off, the police pulled us over—the last thing I remember was being fingerprinted.

I then woke up in a cold sweat and in a state of panic. "Did that really happen?" I asked myself.

Yes, it did happen. I met Jon in the restaurant that day, but we went our separate ways after exchanging phone numbers and a few minutes of small talk outside of the restaurant. Maybe he went to the bar, I don't know. I went back home, however. So, how could it have happened if I went home? Folger (September, 2001) quotes Deutsch as saying that "we have every possible option we've ever encountered acted out somewhere in some universe by at least one of our other selves" (p. 39).

Without going into how Deutsch and other physicists arrive at this conclusion, I *will* say, that like a particle in quantum physics we too can be in more than one place at a time. "Under normal circumstances," says Deutsch, "we never encounter the multiple realities of quantum mechanics. We certainly aren't aware of what our other selves are doing" (p. 40). Well, maybe we aren't, but maybe we are. Was I not dreaming about drinking and using with Jon? Why couldn't the dream be an awareness of my other self? So which is it? Is it two me's in multiple universes, or one me having a dream? Perhaps it is both. It could be what Freud considered a wish fulfillment, or maybe the dream was having me—rather than the other way around. Maybe I was observing my other universe through dream.

As a quondam drug addict, now clean and sober since 7 May 1990, many people's image of me remains what it was before I recovered—a scandalous drug-addicted trickster. This also goes for my old friend Jon, for he too has been a hedonistic, immutable career drug and alcohol addict for at least as long as I have. I have no reason to believe that he is any different now than he was when we ran together years ago. When Jon and I were talking outside of the restaurant, I told him that I have been clean and sober for 14 years and have earned a Ph.D. He looked at me suspiciously, smiled and said, "yeah, right."

There was once a student who taught a frog to jump: Frog, jump, the student commanded, and the frog jumped. The student cut off one of the frog's legs and said: frog, jump, and the frog jumped. He cut off a second leg: frog, jump, and the frog jumped. The same thing happened after cutting off the third leg. When the student cut off the last leg, the frog would not jump. After a moment's thought, the student wrote: After losing all four legs, the frog loses its hearing. The same goes with Jon's thinking when it concerns me. If I could have shown him my diploma, he would have asked "that's nice, who printed it for you?" If I had introduced him to one of my professors, he would have considered it a conspiracy. If I had shown him my transcripts, he would have shrugged his shoulders and said "computer generated, so what?"

Jon would have to personally observe me for a long time before he would be convinced that my recovery, much less my level of education, really existed. I find the frog parable synonymous to the quantum object that doesn't exist until it is observed.

As it turned out, Jon and I stayed in contact and had lunch together periodically. He had just moved back to town when I saw him at the restaurant. A couple of months later, after he had talked with mutual friends from our pasts, then seeing my name in the Barstow College schedule as a psychology instructor, he finally came to believe that what I told him was true.

We were having lunch one day and he asked how I did it. "I've tried a hundred times to clean up," he said, "and I can never do it."

I said, "Jon, did you know that an electron can move from one place to another without having traversed the intervening space?"

He just looked at me shaking his head. He wasn't impressed a bit. "So what! Is this the way educated people answer simple fucking questions?"

I laughed, then I told him about the Project Change program when I was in prison and about shooing my old thoughts away and replacing them with different ones. "By the time I was released," I told him, "I was certain that I was not going to drink or use anymore." I then explained to Jon that between the time I entered the Project Change program and my release from prison, I had recovered. I don't recall when this actually happened. "Like the intervening space of time that the electron doesn't go through, I don't remember going through that intervening space of time," I said. I then explained to Jon that I could not have done it by myself—I had help by attending 12-step meetings.

The vagabond that he is, Jon didn't stay in town much longer. We both grew up in Barstow, so we kept in touch through snail mail and a periodic phone call. I would go for long periods of time before I would hear from him again. He always had a reason for his reticence: "I went back to prison for a while," or "I got involved with a woman," or "I was on the lam." He had been drinking and using for forty years or more. Most people do not believe that he will ever get clean and sober, including me.

Not long ago I got off work at six o'clock in the evening, went home and sifted through my mail, listened to my phone messages, then went to a restaurant for dinner. As I was waiting in line to pay my bill, the man in front of me turned around to leave and we made eye contact. "Wow, is that really you?" We had not seen each other in years. He said, "I've been clean and sober for two years now, John."

I looked at him suspiciously and said, "yeah, right"! Jon was *non compos mentis*—not of a sound mind, for he was an ignominious liar and a jointster, and had been for most of his life. Some people are just hopeless. When Roland H. called Carl Jung and wanted to be treated again for his addiction, Jung told him that his situation was hopeless. The only hope, Jung told him, was if he were the subject of a spiritual experience. In my opinion, even a spiritual experience could never overpower Jon's hopeless addiction and nefarious behavior.

Jon smirked and said, "John, did you know that a manifestation of one quantum object, caused by our observation, simultaneously influences its correlated twin object—no matter how far apart they are?"

"Oh, so now you're clean and sober, *and* I suppose you have a doctorate in quantum physics?" Ironically, I had to meet someone in a bar that day, so I invited Jon to come along. We made small talk and asked about mutual friends, then after I ordered a diet coke, I asked him if he wanted a cocktail. He said, "No, John! I told you—I am clean and sober!"

I smiled, and playing the devil's advocate, I said "just kidding." Then I asked how he did it. He replied: "even though you and I haven't been associating with each other for the last several years, that doesn't mean you weren't still influencing me from-a-distance." Denney (June/August 2002) explains that "proponents of Era III medicine focus upon the nonlocal, action at-a-distance qualities of quantum particles as providing a rationale with which to support the theory that healing can occur between individuals at-a-distance" (pp. 18-23). Jon then said to me, "John, you and I can be thought of as twin quantum objects—cut from the same mold, you might say—John and Jon. And it doesn't matter where I have been geographically, you have definitely been influencing me."

Then I woke up. I laid there for a while, thinking of Jon and hoping that he was okay. As I was getting out of bed, I got a synchronistic phone call. Bad news! It was one of Jon's friends calling to inform me that Jon was killed in a car accident the night before. After talking with my friend's friend, I also found out to my amazement, that Jon had been clean and sober for two years. I was flabbergasted. What a pyrrhic victory over addiction.

Marie Louise von Franz (1992) wrote that "what Jung calls contingence [synchronicity] refers to an accidental but meaningful coming together of an outer and an inner event. He had observed that individuals chiefly experience such coincidence when an archetype is intensively constellated in their unconscious" (p. 186). Was my dream a caveat? I had been feeling squirrely lately, entertaining thoughts of *hedone*—like an orgy with the lovely Aphrodite and the blissful Morpheus. The rebellious *puer* within had been rearing his flighty head lately. Was I not dreaming about Jon being clean and sober for two years? So which is it? Synchronicity, or Jon influencing *me* at-a-distance? Perhaps it's both. Maybe it's some kind of paradoxical wish fulfillment, or maybe the dream was having me.

Some theorist's say that even after someone dies, other copies of him might remain alive somewhere in the multiverse; therefore, maybe we can continue to influence each other in the netherworld of dreams whether we are dead or alive?

Whether there can be anything said *positivistically* concerning the quantum phenomenology of my liminal experience, I couldn't say. I, together with atomic physicists and many other positivists, do agree however, that a quantum particle: (1) can be in two places at the same time, (2) doesn't exist until it is observed, (3) can go from one place to another without going through the intervening space, (4) can influence other particles at a distance.

*   *   *

Is this a true story, or is it confabulation? Is it a tall tale by a seasoned trickster? Maybe it is and maybe it isn't. Or, maybe parts of it are true and maybe parts of it aren't. Does it make any difference whether it's true or not? Such is the state of affairs concerning we tricksters. We are never fully redeemed.

Maybe some people are destined to live by organizing principles that we are unaware of. There may be far more than we would like to admit—that we simply don't know or understand.

Perhaps many of our present theories are wrong.

REFERENCES

Alcoholics Anonymous World Services, Inc. *Alcoholics anonymous: The story of how many thousands of men and women have recovered from alcoholism.* 3rd ed. (1991). New York: Alcoholics Anonymous World Services, Inc.

Alcoholics Anonymous World Services, Inc. *Alcoholics anonymous: The story of how many thousands of men and women have recovered from alcoholism.* 4th ed. (2001). New York: Alcoholics Anonymous World Services, Inc.

Alcoholics Anonymous World Services, Inc. (1984). *Pass it on: The story of Bill Wilson and how the A.A. message reached the world.* New York, NY: Alcoholics Anonymous World Services, Inc. p 383.

Alice. (January, 1996). *How many recover from alcohol and drug abuse annually.* In Go Ask Alice. Retrieved January 5, 2008 from http://www.goaskalice.columbia.edu/0763.html).

Bio. (2005). *Robert Downey Jr. biography.* In Biography.com. Retrieved December 25, 2007 from; http://www.biography.com/search/article.do?id=9542052&page=

Bunker, E. (2000). *Education of a felon.* New York: St. Martins Griffin.

Burns, J. E. (1999). Archetypal psychology and addiction treatment. *Spring 65: A journal of archetype and culture,* p. 19.

Burroughs, W. S. (1977). *Junky.* New York: Penguin.

Burroughs, W. S. Jr. (1984). *Speed.* Woodstock, N.Y.: The Overlook Press.

Carson, R and Butcher, J. N. (1992). *Abnormal psychology and modern life.* New York: Harper Collins.

Cavalli, T.F. (2002). *Alchemical psychology: Old recipes for living in a new world.* New York: Tarcher/Putnum.

Chevigny, B. G. (Ed.). (1999). *Doing time: 25 years of prison writing.* New York: Arcade Publishing.

Clarke, M. (December 2007). Sudden rise in New Jersey Prison Guard Firings. *Prison Legal News,* Vol. 18 No. 12.

Contreras, G. (Speaker), & Cole, R. (Producer). (2000). *Education or incarceration: A panel of the Claremont forum* [Film]. (Available from JusticeVision, 1425 W. 12th St. #262, L.A., CA, 90015)

Corbett, L. (1996). *The religious function of the psyche*. New York: Routledge.

CORK Bibliography. (2003). Spontaneous remission. Retrieved July 6, 2003 fr. http://www.projectcork.org/bibliographies/data/Bibliography_Spontane ous_Remission.html

Cohen, S. *The chemical brain: The neurochemistry of addictive disorders*. Irvin, California: CareInstitute.

Donziger, S. R. (Ed.). (1996). *The real war on crime: The report of the national criminal justice commission*. New York: HarperPerennial.

Durkheim, E. (1912). *The elementary forms of religious life*. New York: The Free Press.

Denney, M. (2002). "Walking the quantum talk." *IONS Noetic Sciences Review*, 60, June - August.

Eliade, M. (1958). *Rites and symbols of initiation: The mysteries of birth and rebirth*. New York: Harper& Row Publishers.

Evans, J. (Ed.). (2001). *Undoing time: American prisoners in their own words*. Boston, MA: Northeastern University Press.

Folger, Tim. (2001, September). Quantum shmantum. *Discover*.

Foucault, M. (1995). *Discipline & punish: The birth of the prison*. New York: Vintage Books.

Frankel, R. (1998). *The adolescent psyche: Jungian and Winnicottian perspectives*. New York: Routledge.

Franklin, B. F. (Ed.). (1998). *Prison writing in 20th century America*. New York: Penguin Books.

Fuocco, M. (January 22, 2006). *Jury unveils intrigue at Allegheny County jail*. In Pittsburgh Post-Gazette. Retrieved January 10, 2008 from http://www.post-gazette.com/pg/06022/642263-85.stm

Gilchrist, C. (1998). *The elements of alchemy*. Rockport, MA: Element Books Limited.

Goldman, A. (1974). *Ladies and gentleman: Lenny Bruce*. New York: Random House.

Goswami, Amit. (1995). *The self-aware universe: How consciousness creates the material world*. New York: G.P. Putnam's Sons.

Grof, C. (1993). *The thirst for wholeness: Attachment, addiction, and the spiritual path*. San Francisco, CA: Harper-Collins publishers.

Grog, S. (2000). *Psychology of the future: Lessons from modern consciousness research*. New York: State University of New York Press.

Halpern, Diane F. (1989) *Thought and knowledge*. Hillsdale N.J.: Lawrence Erlbaum Ass.

Hernstein, R. J., and Wilson, J. Q. (1985). *Crime and human nature*. New York: Simon and Schuster.

Hillman, J. (1979). *Puer papers*. Dallas, TX: Spring Publications, Inc.

Hillman, J. (1997). *Archetypal psychology: A brief account*. Woodstock, Connecticut: Spring Publications, Inc.

Hillman, J. (1970). On senex consciousness. *Spring: An annual of archetypal psychology and Jungian thought*. Dallas, Texas: Spring Publications.

Hyde, Lewis. (1998). *Trickster makes this world: Mischief, myth, and art*. New York: Farrar, Straus and Giroux.

Hynes, W. J., & Doty, W. G. (Eds.). (1997). *Mythical trickster figures: Contours, contexts, and criticisms*. Tuscaloosa, AL: The University of Alabama Press.

James, W. (1958). *The varieties of religious experience*. New York: The Penguin Group.

Johnson, R A. (1991). *Owning Your Own Shadow: Understanding the dark side of the psyche*.   San Francisco: Harper.

Jung, C. (1953). *Two essays on analytical psychology*. New York: Pantheon Books Inc.

Jung, C. (1959). *The archetypes and the collective unconscious*. New York: Pantheon Books Inc.

Kiley, D. (1983). *The Peter Pan syndrome: Men who have never grown up*. New York: Dodd, Mead & Co.

Kinney, J & Leaton, Gwen. (1995). *Loosening the grip: A handbook of alcohol information*. St. Louis: Mosby.

Kipnis, A. (1991). *Knights without armor: A practical guide for men in quest of masculine soul*. Los Angeles, CA: Jeremy P. Tarcher, Inc.

Kipnis, A. (1999). *Angry young men: How teachers, and counselors can help "bad boys" become come men*. San Francisco, CA: Jossey-Bass

Leder, D. (2000). *The soul knows no bars: Inmates reflect on life, death, & hope*. Lanham, MD: Rowman & Littlefield Publishers, Inc.

McGuire, J. (July/August 1993). Primed for crime. *Psychology today*.

Morris, N. & Rothman, D.J. (1995). *The oxford history of the prison: The practice of punishment in western society*. New York: Oxford University Press.

Peele, S. (11/12/2001). *Would legalization of alcoholic drinks to minors decrease or increase underage drinking*? In The Stanton Peele Addiction Web Site. Retrieved December 21, 2007 from www.peele.net/faq/childdrink.html.

Radin, P. (1972). *The trickster: A study in American Indian mythology*. New York: Schocken Books.

Raff, J. (2000). *Jung and the alchemical imagination*. York Beach, Maine: Nocolas-Hays, Inc.

Reutter, D. (December 2007). Pennsylvania county jail system overcrowded, under-regulated. *Prison Legal News*, Vol. 18 No. 12.

Revlin, R. & Mayer, R. E. (1978) *Human reasoning*. Washington D.C.: V.H. Winston & Sons.

Ross, R. (April, 1986). *Three nation umbrella org. to aid Jewish prison inmates, families*. In National Jewish Press. Retrieved December 30, 2001 from www.rickross.com/reference/Jewpris5.html (now defunct).

Samenow, S. E. (1989). *Before it's too late*. New York: Times Books.

Scholem, G. (1996) *On the kabbalah and it's symbolism*. New York: Schocken Books.

Shewan, D. & Davies B. (Eds). (2000). *Drug use and prisons: An international perspective*. Canada: Harwood Academic Publishers.

Still, S. (2002). Prison as shadow. In D. P. Slattery & L. Corbett. (Eds.), *Psychology at the threshold* (pp. 329-338). Carpinteria, CA: Pacifica Graduate Institute Publications.

St. John, W. (2003, August 9). Professors with a past. *The New York Times.*

Storie, M. (October/November 2007). Criminal justice and substance abuse. *NAADAC news: The association for addiction professionals.*

Street, L. (1953). *I was a drug addict.* New York: Random House.

Time-Life (Eds.). (1976). *The gunfighters.* New York: Time-Life Books.

von Franz, M. L. (1980). *Alchemy: An introduction to the symbolism and the psychology.* Toronto, Canada: Inner City Books.

von Franz, M. L. (2000). *The problem of the puer aeternus.* Toronto, Canada: Inner City Books.

von Franz, M. L. (1992). *Psyche and matter.* Boston, Massachusetts: Shambhala Publications, Inc.

Walker, C. J. (1999). *One eye closed the other red: The California bootlegging years.* Barstow, CA: Back Door Publishing

Weil, A. (1972). *The natural mind: A new way of looking at drugs and the higher consciousness.* Boston, MS: Houghton Mifflin Company.

Wills, M. & Carona, M. (2000). *Save my son: A mother and a sheriff unite to reclaim the lives of addicted offenders.* Center City, Minnesota: Hazeldon.

Wilson, James Q. (June 10, 1992). Scholars must expand our understanding of criminal behavior. *The Chronicle of Higher Education.*

Woodman, M. (1982). *Addiction to perfection: The still unravished bride.* Toronto, Canada: Inner City Books.

CPSIA information can be obtained at www.ICGtesting.com
Printed in the USA
LVOW060828140112

263757LV00003B/11/P